This book is offered as an example of what can happen in America when racial tensions cause us to forget to love one another.

1921
Tulsa Race Riot
and the
✚ American Red Cross
"Angels of Mercy"

By Bob Hower
Tulsa, Oklahoma

*Compiled from the memorabilia collection of Maurice Willows,
Director of Red Cross Relief*

Printed in the United States of America
By, Homestead Press, Tulsa, Oklahoma
Cover Design: Keith Crosby

©1993 Robert N. Hower

Dedicated to the memory of Maurice Willows, an "Angel of Mercy"

My grandfather spent his professional life in public service. He was with the American Red Cross in St. Louis when Tulsa asked for help to relieve victims of the 1921 Tulsa Race Riot. The Red Cross policy of assistance following a "man- made" disaster was to change when Mr. Willows was sent to Tulsa as Director of Red Cross Relief.

Mr. Willows brought his family to Tulsa, where his daughter, Maurine, married Forrest Hower, a young man from Kansas. Their children, my two sisters and I, were born in Tulsa.

My sincere thanks to:

William Probes, former Director of the Tulsa Chapter of the American Red Cross, for his cooperation and encouragement. I deeply regret Mr. Probes died before seeing this document completed. I thank the current Director, Roger Dahl and his associates, for their continued support.

Larry Sanders, owner-manager of Tulsa's Homestead Press, his Production Manager, Shawnda Sarasua, Carol Brown, typesetter, and Keith Crosby, owner of Litho Graphics in Tulsa. Without their professional assistance and encouragement this book would not exist.

My sisters, Jean Belding and Pat Farrington, my cousins, Janie Drumheller and James Tate, and my aunt, Betty Martin, for their love and encouragement.

My friends and colleagues at ClearTone Hearing Aid Labs in Tulsa, for helping me afford this endeavor.

F.W. (Steve) Stephenson, for his friendship and advice.

Nina Lane Dunn, for organizing Mr. Willows' collection, making it more workable. Ms. Dunn is the author of "Tulsa's Magic Roots," a pictorial history of early Tulsa, including material from her own family's memorabilia.

Bishop Carlton Pearson, pastor of Higher Dimensions Church in Tulsa for his support.

Alco Laminations, for the quality laminating of the cover.

And the many Tulsans who make my home town such a wonderful place.

1921 Tulsa Race Riot "Angels of Mercy"

CONTENTS

THE RIOT, AND RED CROSS RELIEF.   1 to 107
What happened, as written at the time by those who
witnessed and reacted to America's deadliest race riot.
How The American Red Cross became so involved with
a "man-made" disaster for the first time in its history.

RELIEF DIRECTOR'S VIEW OF THE "DISASTER.   109 to 117
From a family history, written by Mr. Willows,
shortly before his death in 1953

DISASTER RELIEF REPORT.   119 to 225
Official history of the Red Cross Relief effort,
prepared by Relief Director, Maurice Willows

ADDENDUM.   226 to 231
With permission from Ruth Sigler Avery, a chapter from her forthcoming
documentary, "FEAR: THE FIFTH HORSEMAN." A surprising answer
to the question of what happened to Dick Rowland and Sarah Page,
based on Ms. Avery's interview with Rowland's "mother" in 1972.
Ms. Avery believes it to be true.

EPILOGUE.
Inside back cover

Introduction
"I did not write this book!"

It was written at the time by those who survived, reacted to, and reported on America's deadliest riot, the 1921 TULSA RACE RIOT.

I transcribed their stories as they were told in the original letters, newspaper clippings, documents and pictures collected by grandfather, Maurice Willows, Director of Red Cross Relief. I inherited the collection from his daughter, Maurine, my mother.

When rioting, death and devastation caused Tulsa to cry for help, Mr. Willows was sent from Red Cross headquarters in St. Louis. The seven month relief effort was monumental and historic. The Red Cross had relieved strikes and riots before, but this was the first time to become so involved with a "man-made" disaster. Grateful victims referred to Willows and his Red Cross colleagues as, "Angels of Mercy."

Not much has been published about the Tulsa Riot, "better to let sleeping dogs lie." What little has been published does not really tell the Red Cross story. It **will** be told here, along with survivors stories of the riot, in fascinating detail, and "in their own words," transcribed from the original material to make it easier to read. A portion of the original will accompany each story to show where the text came from. Not from me. My few words will be in *italics*.

You might find these stories hard to believe if you think of a race riot as what you saw on television of the 1992 Los Angeles Riot. **This** was a different time. A more deadly time. In 1921, many people, and certainly newspapers, talked and wrote about"negroes," "coloreds," or even "niggers." Rarely "blacks." Never "African Americans."

The Tulsa Race Riot began after a young black man, Dick Rowland, was arrested for allegedly attacking Sarah Page, a white female elevator operator. Many feared a lynching. Rowland was released when Ms. Page refused to file charges against him, but the rioting had started.

From the evening of May 31st, until the afternoon of June 1st, 1921, more Americans killed fellow Americans than probably any time since the Civil War. Estimates of 300 or more can only be estimates because bodies were disposed of in ways to make an accurate count impossible.

Mr. Willows called it a "disaster," not a "riot." His official "Disaster Relief Report" is included here in its entirety, detailing what was done and how every dollar was spent.

Also included here, Mr. Willows' personal account of his Tulsa experience, in which he suggests the alleged "elevator incident" was the **excuse** for the riot, not the **reason.**

The stories herein are, for the most part, presented as Mr. Willows did in his collection, according to the dates they were written. I think you will find them interesting, provocative, shocking, informative, shameful, and sometimes, unbelievable.

Some of the grammar, punctuation and spelling seems wrong today, but it's how they wrote it; including newspaper language too shocking to be used today, and pastor's warnings which could have been written yesterday.

Thank you for your interest.

Bob Hower

1921 Tulsa Race Riot *"Angels of Mercy"*

American Red Cross

The Tulsa Area Chapter of the American Red Cross is pleased to be a part of this historical endeavor, just as we were proud to play a vital role in the aftermath of the 1921 Race Riot. Founded on principles of humanitarianism, impartiality and neutrality, the American Red Cross stands as ready to serve today as it did in 1921.

Under the direction of Maurice Willows, a person who truly exemplified these key principles, the Tulsa Area Chapter responded then — just as it does today —to meeting the needs caused by disaster. And it responded then — just as it does today — with caring and concern.

In the wake of the 1921 Race Riot, the people of the Red Cross often stood alone in their humanitarian mission. Their services were critical in meeting the health and welfare needs of an entire community. Their efforts, especially those of Mr. Willows, should not be forgotten.

While the series of events documented in this book represent a sad and somber chapter in the history of the Tulsa community, the work of the Red Cross shines as a beacon of light and hope. The stories in this book compellingly illustrate the often used phrase "Red Cross for all people." Cultural diversity remains for us an idea of the heart, as well as of the mind. We continue to hold sacred our responsibility to nurture inclusiveness - from making our programs, like disaster services, more responsive to the needs of diverse communities, to assuring that any individual, from any community, feels needed and wanted as part of the Red Cross family.

The legacy of the 1921 Race Riot is, for the Tulsa Area Chapter, a legacy of service and of hope. As we look to the future, the pages of this book remind us that the power of Red Cross lies in the compassion of those of who serve. We are reminded that, no matter how great the tragedy, the Red Cross eases suffering. We will continue to do this. We must do nothing less.

Help Can't Wait

The Riot
and
Red Cross Relief

1921 Tulsa Race Riot   *"Angels of Mercy"*

THE RIOT:

There had been race riots before and there have been since, like that in Los Angeles in the Spring of 1992, but probably none as deadly as the Tulsa Riot in 1921.

From the first shot on the night of May 31st, until afternoon the next day, June 1st, an entire section of town was pillaged and burned to the ground, as fellow Americans killed each other.

This account of that terrible time is told exclusively in the words of those who were there, as they wrote them at the time, and illustrates why the American Red Cross, for the first time in its history, went beyond its previous guidelines to relieve the victims of a "man made" disaster.

1921 Tulsa Race Riot *"Angels of Mercy"*

1921 Tulsa Race Riot *"Angels of Mercy"*

STATEMENT OF ONE OF THE REFUGEES *(J.W. Hughes, City School Principal)*

On the night of May 31, between nine and ten o'clock, someone told me there was a race conflict. I was asked to go down on the street, but after being told that some had gone to the Court House I refused to go, knowing that I could not use any influence with the scattered bunch. On the morning of June 1, I arose, expecting to go to the school house. I did not have any idea that the trouble had reached such a proportion.

At five o'clock a whistle was blown, seven aeroplanes were flying over the colored district, and a Machine Gun was placed in front of my home. I was called to the door by home guards and armed citizens. I was not dressed, but was told to bring my family out. They said if we would obey they would protect us and our property. I was not allowed to go back into the house. I called my wife and son, she came out dressed only in a kimona and shoes. We were ordered to put our hands above our head, marched up Fairview Street, then across the Stand Pipe Hill to Easton Street, where we found automobiles driven by ladies and men.

National Guard placing machine gun

Being Marched to Convention Hall

We were carried to the City Jail, the men were placed in the corridor down stairs, the women were carried up stairs. after so many were crowded into the corridor, we were carried to Convention Hall. Many people cheered and clapped their hands as we were marched four abreast with our hands above our head.

3

1921 Tulsa Race Riot *"Angels of Mercy"*

Negroes being taken to Convention Hall

A man was shot at the door of the Convention Hall while both hands were above his head. Many men who were shot out in the city were brought in the hall and we heard their cries and groans. Namely: Dr. Jackson, Johnson and Stovall. We looked out of the windows, saw our homes go up in smoke. At noon, we were fed with sandwiches and coffee.

In the late afternoon, we were allowed to leave the Convention Hall only when some white person we had worked for would come and vouch for us. Mr Oberholtzer, City Superintendent of Public Schools, came and called for all colored teachers, and we were taken to the old City High School, where I met my wife again. All the lady teachers were taken to the homes of the city principals and cared for nicely. We were allowed to stay in the old High School all night. The next morning, I saw my wife much improved as to her dress. Miss Kimble of the Domestic Science Department of the white High School gave us our breakfast.

Homes Burning

1921 Tulsa Race Riot "Angels of Mercy"

The next morning, without hat or shoes, I was determined to improve my personal appearance and comfort. After much solicitation I was allowed to go under the guard of a soldier down on Main Street to Renberg's Clothing Store. He gave all the colored male teachers a suit of clothes and hat.

In the evening of the first day after the trouble, I was allowed to go out and look over the burned area. Thirty-five blocks, including my home and eight rent houses, were in ashes.

Thirty five city blocks in ashes.

My second night was spent in the Booker T. Washington High School, which had been placed in charge of the Red Cross. Our wives slept on one side of the house on cots and the men on the other side. I was placed temporarily in charge of conditions of the food supply. We lined the people up, many hundreds being in the line, and fed them their meals by allowing them to pass between two tables, on one was sandwiches, the other, coffee. In this way, we gave each his allowance.

In a very short while, the entire High School Plant was made into a hospital, office rooms, distributing rooms, etc., which soon brought a partial temporary relief to the many who were suffering from wounds, hunger, and the need of clothes.

Four hospital wards in High School

1921 Tulsa Race Riot *"Angels of Mercy"*

The stories told by those who came for relief are so freighted with horror, I refrain from repeating them. Many of the sick were forced from home. Those on crutches were compelled to go likewise. A mother giving birth to child was no exception to the rule.

More destruction

A Reconstruction Committee was appointed by the mayor of the city. A like committee was ordered selected by his honor from the remaining negro population. We have been asked to give up the lands on which our homes, business, churches and schools were located and requested to go north and east of the city, buy and rebuild. The only consideration offered us was leave our lots and when they have increased in value, they will sell them and we have the profit thereby. Thus far, we have failed to acquiesce in the recommendation of the request.

J.W. Hughes. Princ. city School.

> A Reconstruction Committee was appointed by the mayor of the city. A like committee was ordered selected by his honor from the remaining negro population. We have been asked to give up the lands on which our homes, business, churches and schools were located and requested to go north and east of the city, buy and rebuild. The only consideration offered us was leave our lots and when they have increased in value, they will sell them and we have the profit thereby. Thus far, we have failed to acquiesce in the recommendation of the request.
>
> *J. W. Hughes. Princ. city School*

Resolutions of the East End Welfare Board.

RESOLUTIONS

On the 31st night in May, 1921, the fiercest race war known to American history broke out, lasting until the next morning, June 1st, 1921. As a result of this regrettable occurrence, many human lives were lost and millions of dollars worth of property were stolen and burned.

Negro district burning

Hundreds of innocent Negroes suffered as a result of this calamity --- suffered in loss of lives, injury from gun-shot wounds and loss of property. Many of us were left helpless and almost hopeless.

Victims searching rubble.

1921 Tulsa Race Riot *"Angels of Mercy"*

We sat amid the wreck and ruin of our former homes and peered listlessly into space.

It was at this time and under such conditions that the American Red Cross-- that Angel of Love and Mercy came to our assistance. This great organization found us bruised and bleeding and, like the good Samaritan, she washed out wounds, and administered unto us.

Constantly, in season and out, since the regrettable occurrence, this great organization, headed by that high class christian gentleman, Mr_____ Willows, has heard our ever cry in this our dark hour and has ever extended to us practical sympathy. As best she could, with food and raiment and shelter she has furnished us. And to this great christian organization our heartfelt gratitude is extended.

Riot victim..

Red Cross staff .... Willows on right.

Therefore be it resolved that we, representing the entire colored citizenship of the city of Tulsa, Oklahoma, take this means of extending to the American Red Cross, thru Mr. Willows, our heart-felt thanks for the work it has done and is continuing to do for us in this our great hour of need.

Resolved further that a copy of these resolutions be sent to the American Red Cross Headquarters, a copy be mailed to Mr. Willows and his co-workers and that a copy be spread upon the minutes of the East End Welfare Board.

         Respectfully submitted.

(SIGNED)

B. C. Franklin	I.N. Spears
E. F. Saddler	P. A Chapelle
J. W. Hughes	Dimpie L. Bush

    Committee.

Photo of original document showing original signatures

1921 Tulsa Race Riot *"Angels of Mercy"*

Copy of the original Handwritten letter from Mayor Evans requesting Red Cross help:

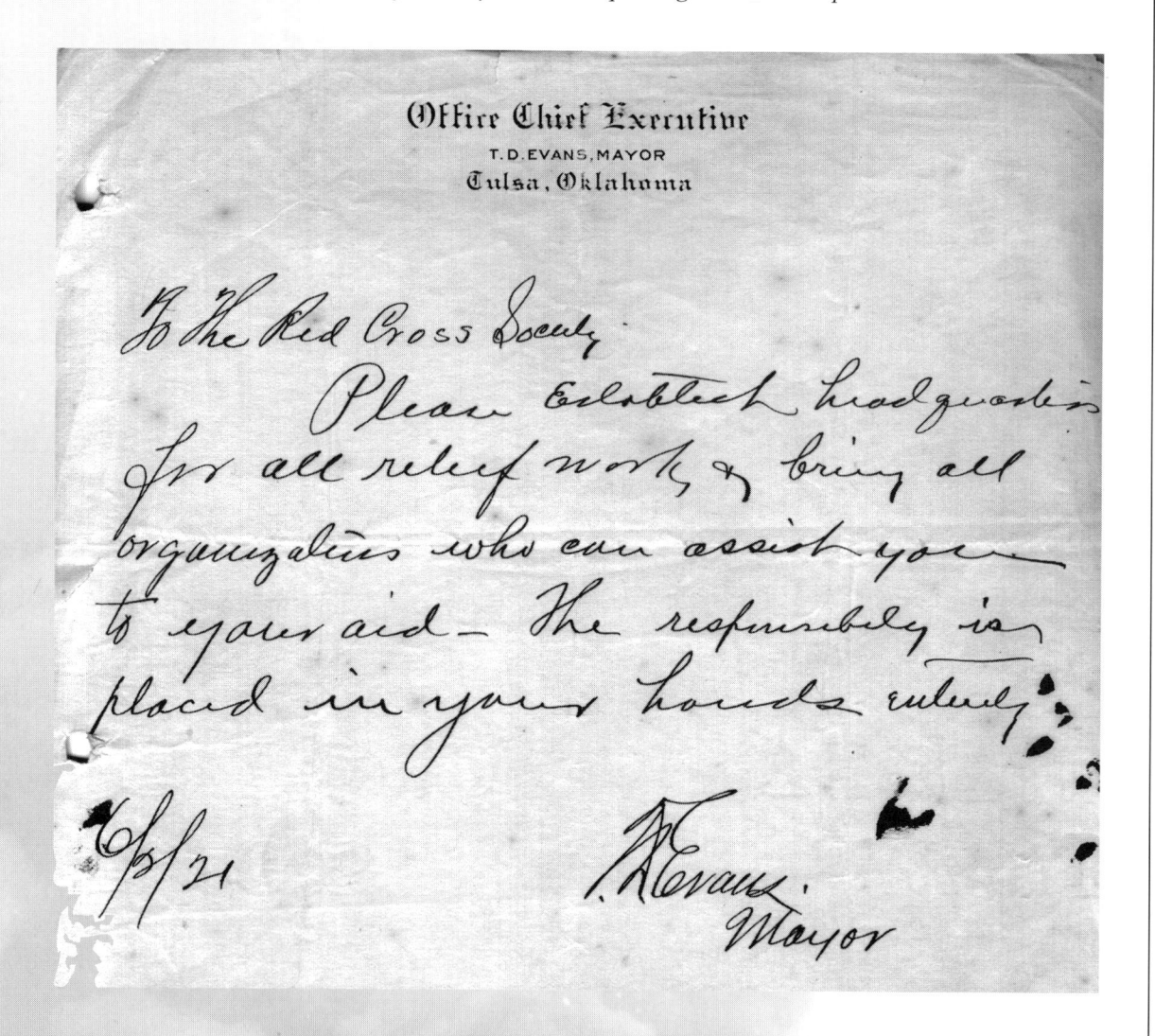

Office Chief Executive
T.D. Evans, Mayor
Tulsa, Oklahoma

To The Red Cross Society

    Please establish headquarters for all relief work, & bring all organizations who can assist you to your aid--- The responsibility is placed in your hands entirely.

6/2/21   T.D. Evans
                                                    Mayor

1921 Tulsa Race Riot "Angels of Mercy"

National Guard Order, June 2, 1921 (With spelling and missing words as shown)

HEADQUARTERS NATIONAL GUARD
CITY HALL, TULSA OKLAHOMA, June 2, 1921

Field order No. 5. To Commanding Officer, 3 infantry. You will detail a Non-Commissioned officer and 12 men to act as guard at Fair Grounds Dention Camp, this detail be armed and fully equipped will report to Clark Field at American Red Cross Headquarters. From and after 1 P.M. this date detention camp at McNulty Camp will abolish and camps will be removed to Detention Camp at Fair Grounds.

By Command of Brig, Gen. Barrett.

Bryon Kirkpatrick

May. A.G. Dept. Adj.

HEADQUARTERS NATIONAL GUARD
CITY HALL, TULSA OKLAHOMA, June 2, 1921.

Field order No. 5. To Commanding Officer, 3 infantry. You will detail a Non-Commissioned officer and 12 men to act as guard at Fair Grounds Dention Camp, this detail be armed and fully equipped will report to Clark Field at American Red Cross Headquarters. From and after 1 P. M. this date detention camp at McNulty Camp will abolish and camps will be removed to Detention Camp at Fair Grounds.

1921 Tulsa Race Riot "Angels of Mercy"

National Guard Order, June 2, 1921 (With spelling and missing words as shown)

HEADQUARTERS OKLAHOMA NATIONAL GUARD
TULSA   OKLAHOMA   JUNE 2, 1921

Field Order No. 4

All the able bodies negor men remaining in detention camp at Fair Grounds and other places in the City of Tulsa will be required to render such service and perform such labor as is required by the military commission and the Red Cross in making the proper sanitary provisions for the care of the refugees.

Able bodied women, not having the care of children, will also be required to perform such service as maybe required in the feeding and care of the refugees.

This order covers any labor necessary in the care of the health or welfare of these people who, by reason of their misfortunes, must be looked after by the different agencies of relief.

By order of Brig. Gen. Chas. F. Barrett-

_____

Chas. F. Barrett
Brig. Gen.

1921 Tulsa Race Riot *"Angels of Mercy"*

13

1921 Tulsa Race Riot *"Angels of Mercy"*

Mt. Zion Baptist Church

1921 Tulsa Race Riot *"Angels of Mercy"*

STATEMENT OF THE PASTORS OF THE CITY OF TULSA

The fair name of the city of Tulsa has been tarnished and blackened by a crime that ranks with the dastardly deeds of the Germans during the Great War, provoked by the bad element of the negroes, arming themselves and marching through the streets of the city. Block after block of our city has been swept by fire applied by the frenzied hand of the mob. Many of our people are dead, while thousands of innocent, peaceable, and law-abiding citizens have not only been rendered homeless, but have been robbed and despoiled of all their earthly possessions. The pastors of Tulsa blush for shame at this outrage which renders our city odious and condemned before the world.

(Continued on next page.)

1921 Tulsa Race Riot "Angels of Mercy"

Original document continues as shown in Mr. Willows' collection.
It is also included in his "DISASTER RELIEF REPORT," later in this book

We believe that the only bulwark of American safety for our liberties, our homes, the peaceful persuits of happiness, of law, order, and common decency, is found in the teaching and living of the high ideals of Jesus Christ,--that without Christ modern civilization cannot bear weight that is being placed upon it, and the crash is inevitable.

We, the Pastors of this city, hold that there cannot be peace, security, happiness, moral conscience, to say nothing of religious development, so long as the following obtain:

1. The Bible, God, Jesus Christ, and the Christian Religion outlawed in the Public Schools. It is only where Christianity has inclalence and power that the Jew and the Infidel are protected. We insist that they have no right to tear down in America that which not only protects them but protects us. The little sop thrown to the Christian forces at Commencement by Prayer and a Sermon is little more than an insult to Christianity.

While the Bible has been outlawed, the Dance has been put in the Public Schools over the protest of hundreds of fathers and mothers who have a conscience on the subject. Certainly it is an established fact that the dance weakens Moral fibre. We therefore demand consideration.

2. A Wide Open Sunday. The amusement houses, parks, and anything else that desires is free to run wide open on the Lord's Day. It was respect for the Lord's Day and the Lord's House that built that sturdy New England civilization which gave the world the Declaration of Independence, the Constitution of the United States, the great Educational Institutions of the Eastern part of the United States, as well as the great Statesmen, Poets, Philosophers, and Philanthropists.

3. Motion Picture houses constantly showing films that are suggestive in Title, Poster, Advertisement, and in actual production on the screen where there is drinking, the use of weapons, the portrayal of lust, the portrayal of the eternal triangle, the breaking of homes, the caracture of the Christian ministry,--until the young and the ignorant get the idea that such is the common order of Society. That in 1919, Tulsa County gave the startling total of 56.8 divorces, an increase of 18.9% over 1917, two years, is food for solid thought.

4. Officials who can see a car parked a foot out of line, but who are blind to Choc-joints, boot-legging, and the like, said to flourish in and about Tulsa.

5. Officials who have already winked at two lynchings, and who had every opportunity of knowing that a third was contemplated hours before the trouble actually began.

6. Criminals who are given their freedom almost immediately after arrest either on worthless bonds, or through some powerful "Friend" at court, or through some other unlawful manner.

7. A certain type of citizenship which openly boasts of violating the Law with respect to the 18th Amendment.

These and other things have created in the minds of some, especially the younger ones, that the Law is nothing and may be violated with impunity and that punishment is a farce.

(Continues on next page).

-2-

We, the Pastors of the City, of Tulsa, urge that a thorough and complete investigation of this outrage be made immediately, and that whereever the guilty ones may be found, and whoever they are, white or black, that a full punishment be meted out. Good citizenship can not condone and tolerate vandalism, looting, and such other lawless acts as both black and white were guilty of May 31st, and June 1st. We believe that the possession of firearms and ammunition, especially rifles, revolvers, and such should be made a felony.

We call upon the Officials, both County and Municipal for a full enforcement of the Law. We call for a readjustment of our Moral and Civic life, placing it on the plain of decency, righteousness and justice.

We appeal to the Christians of Tulsa to be more faithful in exemplifying the true meaning of Christianity in word and deed, to refrain from all questionable practices, and to give themselves over to the practice of Christian virtues and general Christian living.

We appeal to the unaffiliated Church members to take membership at once with their respective Churches, for in so doing they will strengthen the moral fibre of the Community. This is no time to hold aloof.

We also deem it the part of wisdom that there should be a closer cooperation between the religious and business forces of the two races in Tulsa, so that at all times there shall be a better mutual understanding making it possible for both races to work together to achieve the highest ideals. As an example of what we have in mind, we have invited the pastors of the colored churches to associate themselves with the Ministerial Alliance in this city.

We believe most emphatically that the Church is the only hope for the City of Tulsa, and without her moral influence there can be no security no matter how many or what laws are enacted, or how well policed the city may be. The observance of all law depends upon the moral consciousness and the Church is the only Institution in our Society whose sole and only business is the creating of that Moral Consciousness.

The Church stands between Society and destruction. What are you doing for the Church?

TULSA MINISTERIAL ALLIANCE.

1921 Tulsa Race Riot *"Angels of Mercy"*

Tulsa Tribune, date unknown. The first part of this newspaper clipping is missing.

..... the devastated area is fast becoming a city of tents.

General relief headquarters of the Red Cross have been moved from Fourth street and Cincinnati avenue to the Booker T. Washington school on East Easton street. Here clothing, bedding and medical supplies are being dispensed to the negroes who have returned to their homes. The collection points for these articles will remain at the Y.M.C.A. boy's department and the First Baptist church. Those in charge have requested that those who wish to make contributions notify these headquarters instead of bringing the articles. They will be collected later in a systematic manner.

All refugees are being moved today from the downtown churches to the fairgrounds, where arrangements are being made to take care of those who have no place to go.

Precautions will be taken today by the physicians of the city to prevent an outbreak of smallpox or typhoid fever in this camp. The negroes are to be vaccinated and innoculated today as a preventive measure. Shower bath facilities have been installed and other sanitary conveniences provided there. Women of the city are volunteering their services to feed the negroes. A call for more volunteers has been issued.

The old Cinnabar hospital on North Main street is being used to care for the sick and wounded negroes. The nursing is in charge of Miss Rosalind McKay, state supervisor of public health nursing. Her forces were augmented today by eight nurses from other cities.

Negroes at Work.

Under the general direction of Clark Field, Morris Willow, a Red Cross worker from St. Louis, has been placed in charge of the Red Cross activities. This organization is continuing to procure tents, cots, bedding and clothing for the negroes.

1921 Tulsa Race Riot *"Angels of Mercy"*

O. V. Borden, secretary of the Oklahoma---------Agents' association, has been placed in charge of the purchasing department.

Out in the black belt today gangs of negroes are at work clearing away the rubbish and debris from residence lots under the direction of C.A. Border and other American Legion men. Huge trucks are hauling away the useless rubbish and behind the wreckage gangs other gangs are following putting up tents as temporary shelters for the homeless negroes. In the business district the tottering walls of the buildings are being knocked down as a safety measure. In the residence district the health department has taken the precaution to finish burning the remains of dead animals which perished in the flames.

Passing through the burned district the relief workers are impressed with the resemblance of what they see to the devastation left in the wake of a conquering and pillaging army. Those who burned the district overlooked no opportunity to pillage, as the open trunks in the streets with their contents scattered about partially burned bear witness.

The unquenchable humor of the negro race manifests itself even in this dire extremity of the innocent ones who suffered most heavily.

"Dem shooters took $40 out 'o my trunk," one negro woman confided to another today as she was inspecting her house glad to find it standing. "You'all can't blame dem cause dey wasn't gettin' paid nothin' for their work," the other negro sympathized.

All that remains of most of the shacks and little bungalows that dotted negrotown before the riot are bent and twisted iron bedsteads and springs with here and there a blackened chimney and the cement blocks of the foundations of the more pretentious houses. Inside are the charred embers of the frame structures and furniture, and cook stoves and kitchen utensils that would not burn.

Here and there a small orchard can be seen scorched and wilted by the withering fire. Garden plots also are recognizable by the blackened tops of rows and rows of onions and cabbage.

Negroes Home-Coming.

Darkeytown was an unsightly------------ devastation hit it. Most of it is without sanitation or other modern conveniences except gas and water in some districts.

The streets are mere dirt roads and lanes without pavement or sidewalks, turning and twisting every few blocks. The whole district is so different from the city Tulsans think of as their city that it might be in a foreign country as far as any resemblance it may have to the real Tulsa is concerned. The streets were un-named, the houses un-numbered, barns were built in the streets in the same line with the houses, and general confusion instead of order was the predominant characteristic of the district before the flames reduced most of it to charred ruins.

The home-coming of most of the negroes after the harrowing experiences they have passed through since Tuesday night is an unusual spectacle. Fleeing from their homes to the tune of crackling fire and flying bullets from the weapons of white marauders and negro thugs and vandals, the innocent negroes left practically all of their worldly possessions behind them except the scanty attire they wore on their backs. Returning they find ashes and ruin on all sides.

"Lawsy, massy, ain't dis somethin' awful, even de garden am gone," one old negro mammy said to her 10-year-old son as both looked in despair on the remains of their little house to which they had returned after seeking in vain for the husband and father. "De good Lawd sho' has sent terrible punishment on us niggahs! I sho hopes dey kills dem bad niggahs dat is responsible fo' dis misery. Thank de Lawd all de onions ain't gone. Jes de tops scorched. Land sakes, I sho don' know what we's gwine to do."

Want Guilty Punished

Everywhere the negroes are outspoken in their condemnation of the "bad niggers' who have been stirring up trouble and who they admit are responsible for the uprising of the negroes. They want to see the guilty ones punished. Almost without exception every negro who is asked where he was Tuesday night protests strenuously that he was asleep until the shooting started and then ran out of town to the woods. However, some of them show a surprising knowledge of what was going on. The better element among the negroes seems to be stirred up to bring the guilty ones to justice. They seem to realize that their own safety depends on this.

All of the homes in the negro district were not burned. On the fringes of the district next to the white settlements the shacks are still standing. The negroes who live in these are the only cheerful negroes in Tulsa today. In these one and two-room houses 10, 20, or 30 negro men, women and children are being housed. Groups of them congregate on the front porches to discuss their experiences.

"We wuz all asleep when they beginst to shootin' an' de airplanes to swoop down an' den Sam went out to get de calf," one negro woman was explaining to a group of interested listeners.

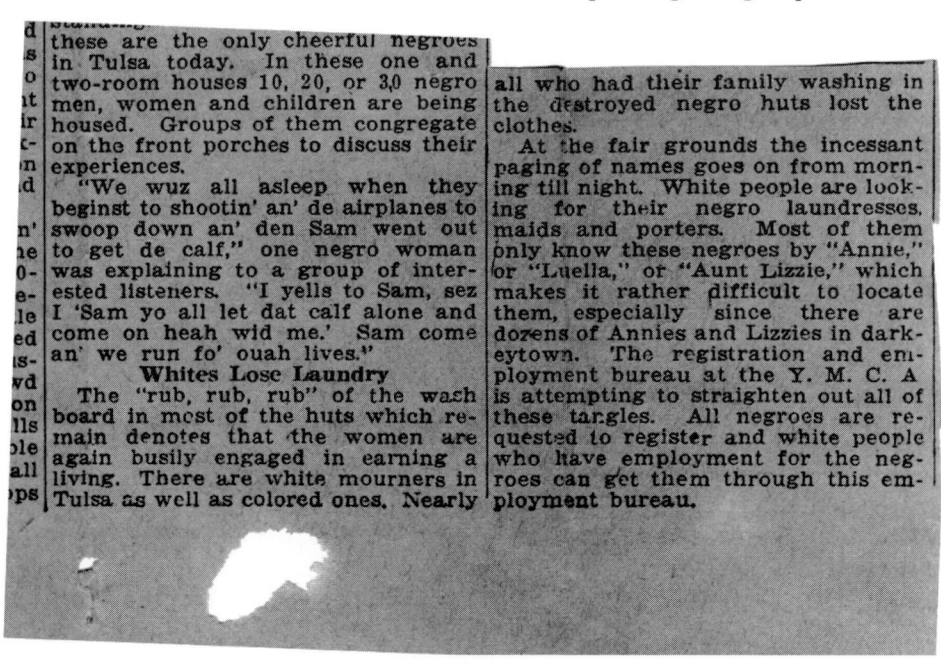

---

these are the only cheerful negroes in Tulsa today. In these one and two-room houses 10, 20, or 30 negro men, women and children are being housed. Groups of them congregate on the front porches to discuss their experiences.

"We wuz all asleep when they beginst to shootin' an' de airplanes to swoop down an' den Sam went out to get de calf," one negro woman was explaining to a group of interested listeners. "I yells to Sam, sez I 'Sam yo all let dat calf alone and come on heah wid me.' Sam come an' we run fo' ouah lives."

Whites Lose Laundry

The "rub, rub, rub" of the wash board in most of the huts which remain denotes that the women are again busily engaged in earning a living. There are white mourners in Tulsa as well as colored ones. Nearly all who had their family washing in the destroyed negro huts lost the clothes.

At the fair grounds the incessant paging of names goes on from morning till night. White people are looking for their negro laundresses, maids and porters. Most of them only know these negroes by "Annie," or "Luella," or "Aunt Lizzie," which makes it rather difficult to locate them, especially since there are dozens of Annies and Lizzies in darkeytown. The registration and employment bureau at the Y. M. C. A is attempting to straighten out all of these tangles. All negroes are requested to register and white people who have employment for the negroes can get them through this employment bureau.

"I yells to Sam, sez I 'Sam yo all let dat calf alone and come on heah wid me.' Sam come an' we run fo' ouah lives."

Whites Lose Laundry

The "rub,rub,rub" of the wash board in most of the huts which remain denotes that the women are again busily engaged in earning a living. There are white mourners in Tulsa as well as colored ones. Nearly all who had their family washing in the destroyed negro huts lost the clothes.

At the fair grounds the incessant paging of names goes on from morning till night. White people are looking for their negro laundresses, maids and porters. Most of them only know these negroes by "Annie," or "Luella," or "Aunt Lizzie," which makes it rather difficult to locate them, especially since there are dozens of Annies and Lizzies in darkeytown. The registration and employment bureau at the Y.M.C.A. is attempting to straighten out all of these tangles. All negroes are requested to register and white people who have work for the negroes can get them through this bureau.

Fairgrounds detention entrance.

EXCHANGE BUREAU BULLETIN

1, Number 33   Tulsa, Oklahoma, July 21, 1921

EVER BUY ANY LUMBER?

Down Red Cross way the other day developments in connection with the temporary rehabilitation program indicated that about one hundred thousand feet of yellow pine lumber would have to be purchased.

Necessarily delivery was the big point involved. However, the prices which had been paid for out-of-stock deliveries on smaller lots recently indicated that everything in the way of price concession, locally, would be tough sledding. And, you tell 'em slaughter house, it was.

Of course it was county money being spent, and should be kept in Tulsa County if possible. On the other hand we have preached at and to the County Commissioners so long and faithfully on the subject of a County Purchasing Agent and how he would save money for the County, that here was our golden opportunity of demonstrating the truth of all we had said.

Our friend Surber is on the job for the Red Cross now and Les proceeded to get some real competitive bids on this order. And that there are some dealers in the United States satisfied with a reasonable margin was very clearly demonstrated.

Of course the local dealers were furnished quotation sheets, and oh boy! a beautiful symmetry was preserved in the quotations received from them. It reminded one, somehow, of that old poem about the charge of the brave six hundred. You know, unbroken ranks, and all that stuff. Perfectly all right, and all that, and what goes up must come down, and where some were up some were down, and—. But we all know. We have been buying lumber for some little time.

But the order was finally "placed" in Tulsa. The County money was kept in Tulsa County and one more Purchaser went home licked but not convinced by any manner of means.

That the law of supply and demand was not properly functioning in this case is evidenced by the fact that for this territory shipments and orders are considerably below production, notwithstanding mill shutdowns.

HOW COMES?

Had you noticed that whenever the City Hall Gang mentions the recent disturbance they call it a "negro uprising," and that whenever a citizen of Tulsa who doesn't owe the Gang anything mentions it, he calls it what it was—a race riot? Funny stunt, an emmisary of the Gang requested the Red Cross to refer to it as a negro uprising, too, in all their reports. But, the Red Cross being one of the most beautifully neutral organizations in the world, politely informed the Gang that the Red Cross had no axes to grind in the matter at all.

1921 Tulsa Race Riot *"Angels of Mercy"*

Exchange Bureau Bulletin, June 2, 1921

RED CROSS PURCHASING DEPARTMENT

The Executive Committee of this Association issued the following instructions on Monday of this week.

"Realizing that this is a time when every citizen of Tulsa should do everything in his power toward the rehabilitation of the city, and appreciating the importance of experienced and technical assistance wherever possible, this committee hereby grants indefinite leave of absence to the Secretary, O.V. Borden, that his services may be available to the Red Cross Organization in establishing and directing a Purchasing Department to handle the purchases of the Red Cross during the continuance of the present grave emergency.

"H.M.COSGROVE, Pres."

O.V. Borden

Exchange Bureau Bulletin June 9, 1921

Tulsa Retains Her Lead

Tulsa has established many records in her time. Some of them most enviable, some otherwise. We made a phenomenal growth as towns and cities are usually credited with growth. We have miles and miles more rotten pavements than most any other village in the world. During war days we raised more money in any less time than other cities many times our size. We can build million dollar hospitals any time we take the notion. When we put on a "race riot" she's a peach.

The one the other day still leaves us far ahead of the field. It is the only one in the history of the world where a policeman or member of the sheriff's force was not injured. Some record!

1921 Tulsa Race Riot "Angels of Mercy"

Tulsa Tribune, June 4th, 1921

Negro Tells How Others Mobilized

The first inside story of what happened in the negro quarter just prior to the time armed bands of blacks swooped down upon the court house and paraded the streets of the business district was told today by O.W. Gurley, one of the wealthiest negroes in Tulsa, who estimates his property loss from fire on Greenwood avenue at close to $150,000.

Gurley declares that the belligerent negroes established headquarters at the plant of the Tulsa Star, published by A.J. Smitherman, early in the evening, assembled ammunition there in large quantities and sent runners hurriedly to all parts of the negro section to round up their forces and bring guns along...

GUARDS READY TO RETURN ON SHORT NOTICE

BARRETT SAYS TROOPS CAN BE RUSHED HERE IN FEW HOURS FROM FT. SILL

That the national guard, 2,500 strong, mobilized for action while in annual encampment at Ft. Sill from June 6 to June 20, will keep a watch full eye upon Tulsa and be ready at a moment's notice to entrain for the city to prevent any threatened disturbance in the near future, was the parting assurance of Adjutant General Charles F. Barrett, as he prepared to leave for Oklahoma City last night.

1921 Tulsa Race Riot "Angels of Mercy"

Tulsa Tribune, Monday, June 4, 1921

Emergencies come when every citizen is expected
to be a good soldier. -- Gen. Wheeler.

RESTORE PEACE

The Committee on Public Welfare has the city well guarded and there is little cause for any anxiety of any further trouble. But it is the duty of every citizen to appreciate the fact that in the aftermath of any such disaster as Tulsa has experienced there is just cause for police vigilance and that it is perfectly proper for the police forces in power to question any person. Any person who is asked to halt to be questioned or searched should immediately be obedient to such request. Every person contributes to the readjustment of normal conditions and of peace by being obedient to every request of any police officer.

The way to build peace now is to be peaceable and have full respect for the authority of all officers of the law. If everybody will go about his work in a peaceful manner and do all he can to re-establish the full sense of peace in invested authorities Tulsa is going to come out all right.

GOOD WORK

The Oklahoma National Guard deserves much praise for its promptness and efficiency in meeting the emergency needs of Tulsa. It brought its men from Oklahoma City here with true military dispatch and held in readiness supplemental forces in nearby cities.

The American Legion, working under the police department and Colonel Hurley's volunteer forces, are also deserving of the people's gratitude for the aid they are now giving at this time.

1921 Tulsa Race Riot *"Angels of Mercy"*

Tulsa Tribune, June 4th, 1921

RED CROSS IN FIELD UNTIL ALL ARE WELL

Temporary Relief to Go On For Months

A total of $5,697.50 was reported at noon today Cyrus S. Avery, treasurer of the reconstruction fund, as having been contributed for this work. The World turned over from its fund $4,942.50 of this amount. The balance of $755 was sent in to Mr. Avery direct.

Funds for relief work are slow in coming in, according to Grant R. McCullough, chairman of the finance committee, who authorized the following statement:

"The funds for the immediate relief of the needy and indigent must be at once.Contributions to date have been distressingly small.

"As chairman of the finance committee of the executive welfare organization, having charge of the restoration work in Tulsa, I earnestly appeal to you for immediate and generous contributions.

"Make checks payable to Cyrus S. Avery, treasurer of the committee, and mail them immediately to box 1851. or deliver at 323-324 Mayo building."

"With the coming of Director Willows from St. Louis to take charge of the organization work here we have the situation well organized now," Clark Field, general director of the temporary relief committee said this morning.

"The temporary relief work will have to be carried on for about 30 days at the Booker T. Washington school even after the negroes return to their homes and temporary shelters. I think that we will be able to close the relief camp at the fair grounds in another week.

"The wounded negroes in the Cinnabar hospital will have to be cared for for several months until they are well. The purchasing of supplies is all systematized now and we have things going in an orderly manner. We are not interfering with the work of the general permanent relief committee and for that reason are not putting up tents in the burned area but are leaving that to the other committee."

Tents Springing Up.

With the concentration of the efforts of the Red Cross and the citizens' reconstruction committee on the task of providing temporary shelter in the................*Rest of article is missing.*

TULSA MUST RESTORE

All citizens of Tulsa are earnestly urged by the Board of Public Welfare to make immediate and generous contributions to the Relief and Restitution Fund and that these monies or checks be sent to Cyrus S. Avery, Treasurer, P. O. Box 1851, or delivered to his offices, Rooms 323 and 324 Mayo Building, Tulsa.

BOARD OF PUBLIC WELFARE.
L. J. MARTIN, Chairman,
GRANT R. M'CULLOUGH,
DR. S. G. KENNEDY,
CYRUS S. AVERY,
H. L. STANDEVEN,
H. C. TYRELL,
MAJ. C. F. HOPKINS,
Executive Committee.

For the convenience of our readers, we ask that this coupon be filled out and attached to check, money order or money so sent:

Cyrus S. Avery, Treasurer,
P. O. Box 1851, or,
323-4 Mayo Building,
Tulsa, Oklahoma.
Please find enclosed $.............. to apply to the Tulsa Relief and Restitution Fund.
Name ....
Address ....

Tulsa Tribune, June 4, 1921

Looking for His Family.

Many Tulsans are assisting to reunite negro families that have become separated in the process of internment. R. E. Love, negro, has searched for his family since Wednesday morning. He has not seen or heard from his wife and four children, one a baby a month old. Mrs. M. R. Travis of 1702 South Boulder, who is in charge of this case, is anxious to hear from anyone who knows of the whereabouts of Mrs. Love and the children. Her telephone number is Osage 2447.

• •

A ride through the burned district yesterday afternoon revealed many groups of able-bodied negroes standing about in more or less careless mood. Mayor Evans' edict to work or face vagrancy charges should change this situation.

• •

A man's home is his castle-- in Oklahoma the same as elsewhere. An officer without a search warrant has no more right to invade it than a professional burglar. If the search warrant is not available, then it is the duty of the police to exercise common sense in their selection of houses that might justify a search.

• •

The suggestion of the Real Estate Exchange that the negro district be moved out farther, the present burned-over area to be given over to industry and switch tracks is a sensible one. If Tulsa business is to expand, the ground occupied by the section now in ashes is by all odds one of the most necessary to such expansion.

• •

The honor of a large number of Tulsans is being put to the test by the gun store men. They want their property returned.

Tulsa Tribune, June 7, 1921

• •

VOTE TO PAY RIOT BILL.

City Passes Measure for First $37,692 Debt.

The appropriation of $37,692.53 from the funds declared to be available in the city treasury to pay the extra policemen and other expenses incident to the situation brought about by the race riot last week was made by the city commission this morning.

This budget will have to be approved by the county excise board before it is legal. A meeting of that body was requested by the commission for this purpose. It will meet in 10 days from today.

Tulsa Tribune, June 4th, 1921

HOSTESS HOUSE FOR NEGROES IS BEING ERECTED

COLORED LEADERS OF NATION CALLED HERE TO HELP IN RELIEF PLANS

A complete plan of helpful service through colored community centers for the purpose of preventing unrest, idleness and disease among colored women has been undertaken by the Y.W.C.A., which has summoned the best avvailable aid from its national and regional headquarters to carry through the program with dispatch. The first step in this work will be the opening Monday morning of a Hostess House for colored women in a building at 123 E. Archer St., turned over to the Y.W.C.A. for that purpose by J.D. Render of the Riwtway Laundry.

This house, which will include services of bath, disinfection, sewing and restrooms and employment registration, will be supplanted within 30 or 60 days by a large new Hostess House built on war-time plans on a lot at the corner of East Archer and North Cincinnati avenue. The site has been donated by Charles Page, who also has placed strip lath to cover half of the building at the disposal of the Y.W.

Plans for the temporary and permanent community centers to be operated under Y.W. auspices have been rushed through by Miss Harriett Pyle, general secretary of the local association, and Miss Harriett Vance, city field secretary for the southwestern district, who arrived from Dallas today.

Miss Cordella Wynn, national colored field secretary of the Y.W., will leave New York tonight for Tulsa to assume full charge of the work here.

Semi-Permanent Structure

Ben Lancaster and Frank Townsend already have volunteered their services to supervise the construction and securing of materials for the new Hostess House, which is planned to serve the needs of colored women and girls for a period of a year or two. Townsend is drawing up plans for a building 100 by 120 feet of the large hut type, and will receive all donations of materials used in the erection and equipment of the house, and offers to supply materials should be made to him at once, is it announced by the Y.W. leaders.

The furnishing of the house, including curtains, carpets, chairs, furniture, kitchen equipment and recreation facilities, also must be accomplished by donations from merchants and individuals. Offers to supply this type of commodities will be received at the Y.W.C.A., phone Osage 6136. In the new house there will be a large community room for resting or dining purposes, employment offices, sewing and work rooms, bath and shower rooms, and ten dormitories for two girls each.

The police department and military authorities already have assured the Y.W. full protection day and night for both the temporary and permanent hostess houses. Mrs. Julia Jackson and Mrs. Howard, colored women, are to take charge of the temporary quarters late today and will be actively supervising the work there with a corps of trained assistants from the groups of colored Y.W. workers.

Need Many Jobs

The task of securing employment for hundreds of colored girls and women will be the first one assumed at a meeting next week. The house will be a clearing bureau for employment and will receive calls for colored women from the city and other points.

Charles Page has offered rooms in Sand Springs for 150 colored girls as fast as they find employment in Tulsa, and will provide free transportation for them on the interurban cars. The problem of the younger colored girls will also be met by the Y.W. by the establishment of a colored girls' summer camp, two miles west of Sand Springs, for which Mr. Page has donated the site. Miss Marguerite Rhodes, a graduate of the Sargent Physical Training school, is on her way to Tulsa now to assume charge of the recreation work and summer camp for colored younger girls.

The labor used in building the new Hostess House must be paid a living wage, and it is the plan of Miss Pyle that unemployed negro men be given this work, the compensation for them to be advanced by money donations from the public. Checks for this work should be sent to Miss Edna Pyle at the Y.W.C.A., marked Labor Fund. Mrs. J.A. Hull, Mrs. B.L. Love, and Miss Florence Heald compose the active committee of the Y.W.C.A. volunteer workers which has charge of centralizing outside assistance for this job.

Tulsa Tribune, June 4th, 1921

SUB-STATION OF POSTOFFICE IS RAZED BY FIRE

ONE VIOLATION OF FEDERAL LAWS UNCOVERED BY SECRET SERVICE AGENT

Immediately following orders by Attorney General Daugherty for a general federal investigation into the race riot, Secret service Officer Weis arrived here from Oklahoma City yesterday to conduct an inquiry, which developed that the United States post office sub-station at 108 N. Greenwood av., was burned, constituting at least one infraction of a federal law.

Officer Weis is reported to have returned to Oklahoma City today but it is understood the directions of Attorney General Daugherty to conduct a general inquiry will be carried out in detail before the matter is regarded as closed by the government.

Deputy United States Marshal W. N. Ellis said the parties who burned the postoffice building and contents would be subject to federal prosecution involving a penitentiary sentence should they be apprehended and found guilty.

Postal authorities said today that the monetary loss at the substation was slight. A check shows that Postmaster A.F. Bryan, of the sub-station, had but $80 worth of equipment on hand and $23 worth of this was recovered. No mail bags were at the station when it burned. There were a number of letters deposited for transmission and several money orders, the loss of which Postmaster Crutchfield's office said the government would make good. The building was private property.

1921 Tulsa Race Riot "Angels of Mercy"

Tulsa Tribune Editorial Saturday, June 4, 1921

The moment that law is destroyed, liberty is lost; and men, left free to enter upon the domains of each other, destroy each others' rights, and invade the field of each other's liberty.
Timothy Titcomb.

IT MUST NOT BE AGAIN

Such a district as the old "Niggertown" must never be allowed in Tulsa again. It was a cesspool of iniquity and corruption. It was the cesspool which had been pointed out specifically to the Tulsa police and to Police Commissioner Adkison, and they could see nothing in it. Yet anybody could go down there and buy all the booze they wanted. Anybody could go into the most unspeakable dance halls and base joints of prostitution. All this had been called to the attention of our police department and all the police department could do under the Mayor of this city was to whitewash itself. The Mayor of Tulsa is a perfectly nice, honest man, we do not doubt, but he is guileless. He could have found out himself any time in one night what just one preacher found out. In this old "Niggertown" were a lot of bad niggers and a bad nigger is about the lowest thing that walks on two feet. Give a bad nigger his booze and his dope and a gun and he thinks he can shoot up the world. And all these four things were to be found in "Niggertown" -- booze, dope, bad niggers and guns.

The Tulsa Tribune makes no apology to the Police Commissioner or to the Mayor of this city for having plead with them to clean up the cesspools in this city.

Commissioner Adkison has said that he knew of the growing agitation down in "Niggertown" some time ago and that he and the Chief of Police went down and told the negroes that if anything started they would be responsible.

That is first class conversation but rather weak action.

Well, the bad niggers started it. The public would now like to know: why wasn't it prevented? Why were these niggers not made to feel the force of the law and made to respect the law? Why were not the violators of the law in "Niggertown" arrested? Why were they allowed to go on in many ways defying the law? Why? Mr. Adkison, why?

The columns of The Tribune are open to Mr. Adkison for any explanation he may wish to make.

These bad niggers must now be held, and, what is more, the dope selling and booze selling and gun collecting must STOP. The police commissioner, who has not the ability or the willingness to find what a preacher can find and who WON'T stop it when told of it, but merely whitewashes himself and talks of "knocking chairwarmers" had better be asked to resign by an outraged city.

SATURDAY, JUNE 4, 1921.

The moment that law is destroyed, liberty is lost; and men, left free to enter upon the domains of each other, destroy each other's rights, and invade the field of each other's liberty.—Timothy Titcomb.

IT MUST NOT BE AGAIN

SUCH a district as the old "Niggertown" must never be allowed in Tulsa again. It was a cesspool of iniquity and corruption. It was the cesspool which had been pointed out specifically to the Tulsa police and to Police Commissioner Adkison, and they could see nothing in it. Yet anybody could go down there and buy all the booze they wanted. Anybody could go into the most unspeakable dance halls and base joints of prostitution. All this had been called to the attention of our police department and all the police department could do under the Mayor of this city was to whitewash itself. The Mayor of Tulsa is a perfectly nice, honest man, we do not doubt, but he is guileless. He could have found out himself any time in one night what just one preacher found out.

In this old "Niggertown" were a lot of bad niggers and a bad nigger is about the lowest thing that walks on two feet. Give a bad nigger his booze and his dope and a gun and he thinks he can shoot up the world. And all these four things were to be found in "Niggertown"—booze, dope, bad niggers and guns.

The Tulsa Tribune makes no apology to the Police Commissioner or to the Mayor of this city for having plead with them to clean up the cesspools in this city.

Commissioner Adkison has said that he knew of the growing agitation down in "Niggertown" some time ago and that he and the Chief of Police went down and told the negroes that if anything started they would be responsible.

That is first class conversation but rather weak action.

Well, the bad niggers started it. The public would now like to know: why wasn't it prevented? Why were these niggers not made to feel the force of the law and made to respect the law? Why were not the violators of the law in "Niggertown" arrested? Why were they allowed to go on in many ways defying the law? Why? Mr. Adkison, why?

The columns of The Tribune are open to Mr. Adkison for any explanation he may wish to make.

These bad niggers must now be held, and, what is more, the dope selling and booze selling and gun collecting must STOP. The police commissioner, who has not the ability or the willingness to find what a preacher can find and who WON'T stop it when told of it, but merely whitewashes him-

1921 Tulsa Race Riot *"Angels of Mercy"*

Tulsa Tribune, June 5, 1921

TOTAL LOSS IN FIRE IS FIXED AT $1,500,000

503 RESIDENCES RAZED BY FLAMES; BUSINESS DISTRICT LOSS $500,000

An estimate of the property loss in the negro district, resulting from the rioting and fire Wednesday morning, was made by real estate men last night, placing the figures at between $1,500,000 and $2,000,000.

destroyed by fire was made by The Tribune yesterday, revealing the fact that 503 houses were completely destroyed. These houses, not including business buildings, were valued all the way from $100 to $4,500. Mervitt J. Glass, president of the Real Estate exhange, says that he considered the average value of these houses at about $1,000, thus making a total of $500,000. He valued the clothing, furniture and other personal property of the average home at $500, or a total of $250,000.

East Side of Greenwood Avenue showing former businesses

An estimate of the property loss in the negro district, resulting from the rioting and fire Wednesday morning, was made by real estate men last night, placing the figures at between $1,500,000 and $2,000,000.

An actual count of the residences

The property loss in the business district has been placed at about $500,000 for buildings and fixtures by the real estate men, and the stocks of goods at $250,000 by R.G. Dun & Co. Higher estimates plased on the business property and personal property of the

34

West side of Greenwood Avenue showing former businesses

negroes by individual real estate men makes the total vary between $1,500,000 and $2,000,000.

Check Being Made

This is the most accurate estimate obtainable until the real estate men complete their present task of listing the property losses. They are doing this as fast as possible maintaining headquarters in the burned area where all losses are being reported.

This committee has been enlightened to a considerable extent by the claims already made by the negroes. One negro, who lived in a $600 house, said that his clothing and personal property was worth $1,500. Mr. Glass last night stated that it was not unusual for them to have clothing and personal property worth much more than the houses in which they lived.

"One negro had a $225 cook stove and a $300 bed room suite," Mr. Glass said.

"They like to dress well and a good many of them are turning in claims for five and six suits of clothes and silk shirts. They seem to care more for what they wear than anything else."

(remainder of article is missing)

Recommendations of Doctors Committee:

Tulsa or Oklahoma Hospitals.

    Red Cross Hospital-- Dr. R.V. Smith and Assistants shall have charge of all operative cases at the Morningside and Red Cross Hospitals. Dr. C.H. Haralson and assistants shall take care of all eye, ear, nose and throat cases arising anywhere which may require special attention and those now in or coming to the Morningside or Red Cross Hospitals.

    Booker Washington first Aid Station-- Dr. Geo. H. Miller, Dr. C.S. Summers and assistants shall be responsible for the first aid and after treatment of all cases applying to this dispensary.

    The Committee recommends that no attempt be made to rebuild the devastated area until a sanitary sewerage system has been installed, with connections to each building or that it shall at least be started and no building planned without such connections and accessories, within the corporate limits of the City.

Wooden shack is temporary home.

    We further recommend that the adjacent territory now situated in the County, be immediately included within the corporate limits in order that the health of the community may be protected by the installation of proper sewerage.

    We further recommend that recognizing the extremely insanitary conditions existing within the devastated area, that if legally possible, the same be corrected through condemnatory proceedings and necessary destruction of all shacks that are now a menace to health.

Tent with wooden sides as temporary housing.

In view of the fact that their building and equipment have been destroyed by fire, we recommend that temporary quarters be provided in the colored district for the use of the Tulsa County Public Health A'ssn., that its work may be resumed at once and we further recommend that permanent quarters be provided as soon as possible. We further recommend that the tuberculosis and general public health work be resumed at once among the white population at the Public Health dispensary, 15 West 11th St.

By order of the Committee

    Dr. C.L. Reeder, Chairman

    Dr. R.V. Smith

    Dr. Horace T. Price, Secy.

1921 Tulsa Race Riot *"Angels of Mercy"*

The Physicians Committee selection of Department Chiefs:

Tulsa, Okla.
June 5th, 1921

The Physicians Committee of the Board of Public Health recognises and accepts the selection of Chief of Departments as made by the American Red Cross as follows, i.e.

Surgery	Dr.. Ralph V. Smith
Obstetrics	Dr. George R. Osborn
Medicine	Dr. Horace T. Price

For immediate service the following Doctors may be called:

Surgery	Dr. H. D. Murdock	0 - 95
	Dr. A. W. Pigford	0 - 187
	Dr. H. S. Browne	0 - 1039
	Dr. C. D. Johnson	0 - 5011
	Dr. G. H. Miller	0 - 6669
Medicine	Dr. A. G. Wainwright	0 - 497
	Dr. C. S. Summers	0 - 9160
	Dr. W. J. Trainor	0 - 8744
	Dr. J. E. Wallace	0 - 812
	Dr. E. B. Wilson	0 - 872
Obstetrics	Dr. Geo. R. Osborn	0 - 2010

It is the purpose of this committee to work in harmony with the American Red Cross and the other organizations doing relief work.

In recognition of the valuable services performed by Dr. Paul R. Brown, we recommend that in case of need he be consulted by all chiefs of departments and this committee.

The committee requests that the various types of work outlined further on, at the places named be performed by the designated physicians.

Sanitation - Dr. C. L. Reeder, Dr. L. C. Presson and assistants shall be responsible for sanitation throughout the city and county.

Fair Grounds Camp - Dr. C. D. Johnson, A. G. Wainwright and assistants shall have charge of all medical and surgical cases at the Fair Grounds Camp, but sending all Major operative cases to the Morningside Hospital and others requiring hospitilization to the Red Cross Hospital.

Obstetrics - Dr. Geo. R. Osborn and Assistants shall take care of all obstetrical cases arising anywhere, which must be sent in time to the *??? (end of original document)*

1921 Tulsa Race Riot *"Angels of Mercy"*

This picture taken at the "The Red Cross hospital" referred to in this document. This was at the Booker T. Washington high school, three days after the riot. The person leaning against the porch railing is Red Cross Relief Director, Maurice Willows. The other unidentified gentleman in the photo is possibly one of the Doctors mentioned in the Physicians Committee Report on the previous page.

> responsible for sanitation throughout the city andcounty.
>
> Fair Grounds Camp - Dr. C.D. Johnson, A.G. Wainwright and assistants shall have charge of all medical and surgical cases at the Fair Grounds Camp, but sending all Major operative cases to the Morningside Hospital and others requiring hospitilization to the Red Cross Hospital
>
> Obstetrics - Dr. Geo. R. Osborn and Assistants shall take care of all obstetrical cases arising anywhere, which must be sent in time to the

Final paragraph from original document, showing abrupt ending as seen on previous page.

AMERICAN RED CROSS
(Disaster Relief Headquarters)

✚

Tulsa County Chapter

Tulsa, Oklahoma

Physicians Service at Booker Washington School

Tuesday	All morning	J. Smitherman
	Afternoon	B.A. Wayne
	All night	A.F. Bryant
Wednesday	A.M.	J. Smitherman
	P.M.	Bridgewater
	Night	B.A. Wayne
Thursday	A.M.	A.F. Bryant
	P.M.	Smitherman
	Night	Wayne
Friday	A.M.	Bryant
	P.M.	Smitherman
	Night	Bridgewater
Saturday	A.M.	Wayne
	P.M.	Bryant
	Night	Smitherman
Sunday	A.M.	Bridgewater
	P.M.	Bryant
	Night	Wayne

Red Cross Physicians Schedule at Washington high school.

AMERICAN RED CROSS
(Disaster Relief Headquarters)

✚

Tulsa County Chapter

Tulsa, Oklahoma

Physicians Service at Fairgrounds

Day / Hours	Physicians
Tuesday 11 A.M. to 4 P.M. All night) 8 P.M. to 8 A.M)	Wells Wickham
Wednesday 11 to 4 Night	Whitley Key
Thursday 11 to 4 Night	Wells Mottey
Friday 11 to 4 Night	Sneed Wickham
Saturday 11 to 4 Night	Mottey Whitley
Sunday 11 to 4 Night	Key Wells

Red Cross Physicians Schedule at fairgrounds.

Tulsa tribune, June 5th, 1921

'GIVE AT ONCE' AVERY'S PLEA TO SAVE CITY

FUND TOTAL IS LESS THAN $9,000; SIX FIGURES NEEDED

Approximately $9,000 had been turned into the coffers of the Public Welfare Fund for relief and reconstruction among sufferers in the burned area at the last accounting yesterday. Subscriptions were not being received in the number which the board must receive them if the immense work of feeding and housing several thousand homeless negroes is to go unhampered, Cyrus S. Avery, treasurer of the board declared.

"We can only appeal to every citizen to make a generous subscription without delay," said Mr. Avery last night. "These funds are not needed for any sentimental purpose or for pampering or favoring anybody. They are absolutely necessary for buying food and shelter and plain necessities of life for about 5,000 negroes now charges on this city.

"The Public Welfare Board has not yet defintely outlined its policy of finance and contribution payments, but there is no doubt about the money being needed badly in large amounts for temporary relief alone. And whatever plan is adopted, we shall have to have not hundreds of dollars but hundreds of thousands of dollars before this restoration work is complete, even in the most primary sense. All donations are carefully recorded, and if there should be any surplus, the amount will be prorated and returned. But at present there is only one thought in front of us -- get the job done that is right before us and pay for it."

Avery stated that about 500 negroes still are camping in the concentration center at the free fair grounds, where meals are now being prepared under their own direction. Scores of colored folks are back in their own neighborhood living in tents, however, for the Red Cross erected a tent city near the Booker T. Washington school late yesterday to afford housing and relieve congestion at the fair grounds.

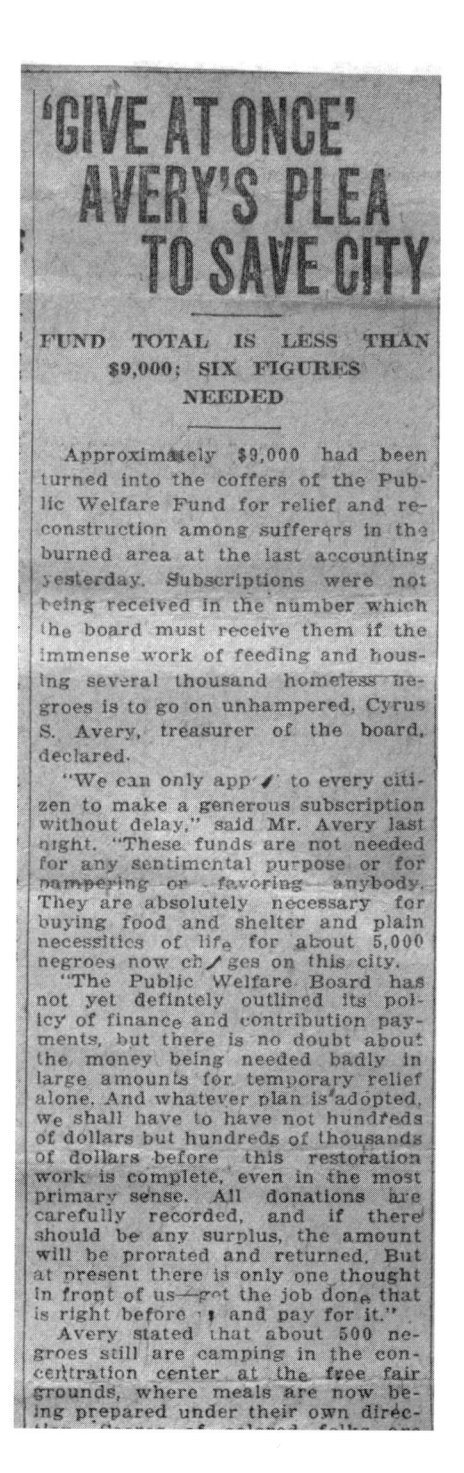

1921 Tulsa Race Riot *"Angels of Mercy"*

(In his official report, Red Cross Relief Director, Maurice Willows, says:
"The number of dead is a matter of conjecture. Some knowing ones estimate the number of killed as high as 300, others estimates being as low as 55. The bodies are hurriedly rushed to burial, and the records of many burials are not to be found. For obvious reasons this report cannot deal with this subject,"

Tulsa Tribune, June 5th, 1921

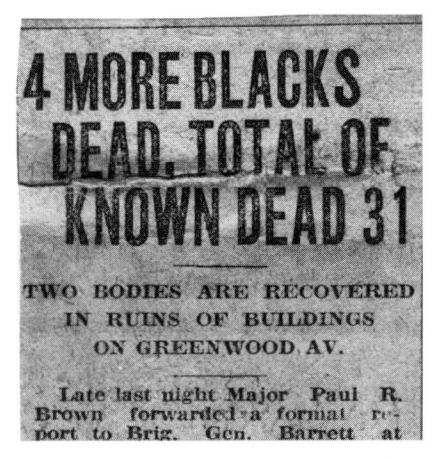

4 MORE BLACKS DEAD. TOTAL OF KNOWN DEAD 31

TWO BODIES ARE RECOVERED IN RUINS OF BUILDINGS ON GREENWOOD AV.

Late last night Major Paul R. Brown forwarded a formal report to Brig. Gen. Barrett at Oklahoma City fixing the number of dead at 36, 10 whites and 26 negroes. The report lists as slightly wounded, 63 whites, 166 negroes; severely wounded 16 whites, 72 negroes. These figures fixing the total number of dead are at variance with the death list compiled by the Tribune as shown in the following story.

The known death list of race riot victims was

Workers gathering bodies.

increased to 31 yesterday with the uncovering of the charred remains of two negroes in the ruins of the business buildings on North Greenwood avenue.

Ten white men and boys lost their lives in the riot and the most accurate list of negro dead obtainable until today was 18. Fifteen of these bodies were taken to the Stanley-McCune and three to Mowbray's morgue. Mowbray reported last night that four negroes had been burried by them and that today the body of another negro was brought in burned beyond recognition. Another body similarly burned was taken to Stanley-McCunes. None of the negro undertakers have opened their establishments since Tuesday night when the riot broke.

"Burned beyond recognition."

With the discovery of these two bodies city authorities considered it highly probable that the bodies of other victims might be discovered in the ruins of the negro hotels and business buildings.

11 Whites in Hospitals

A negro named George Hawkins died at the Cinnabar hospital Saturday but it was said there that he was brought here unconscious from Red Fork and died from natural causes and not from injuries or wounds received in the riot.

Eleven white persons injured in the riot, are still being taken care of in local hospitals. Mrs. S.A. Gilmore, 225 E. King St., is the most seriously injured. She was shot several times in the arm. The others are in less serious condition. At the Cinnabar hospital 47 negroes were being taken care of last night, nearly all of whom were wounded in the riot. About half of these are considered to be in a serious condition. Friday 72 negroes were being taken care of there but a number were discharged and others went to the homes of their friends and relatives.

The Chicago (Defender), Saturday, (probably in October, 1921)

Officer of Law Tells Who Ordered Aeroplanes to Destroy Homes

Tulsa, Okla. Oct. 14 -- Elisah Scott of Topeka, Kan., one of the attorneys retained by the Tulsa riot victims, has a signed affidavit in his possession that when produced will throw an entirely new light on the insurrection carefully planned by the whites here on May 31 last.

It is the confession of a former Tulsa policeman, Van B. Hurley (white), and consists of 31 pages. Hurley, who was honorably discharged from the force and given splendid recommendations by his captains and lieutenants, names several prominent city officials who he declared met in a downtown office and carefully planned the attack on the segregated district by the use of airplanes. He gives in detail a description of the conference between local aviators and the officials.

After this meeting Hurley asserted the airplanes darted out from hangars and hovered over the district dropping nitroglycerin on buildings, setting them afire. When questioned regarding instructions from police officials shortly before the riot, his answer was as follows: "They gave instructions for every man to be ready and on the alert and if the niggers wanted to start anything to be ready for them. They never put forth any efforts at all to prevent it whatever, and said if they started anything to kill every b____ son of a b____ they could find." Gustafson, who was chief of police at the time, was later dismissed.

"On the morning of June 1 they gave me orders to go over to the Negro district," Hurley said. "There was a bunch of rogues, the lower class of white people, stealing and robbing and bursting open trunks and carrying off stuff. Well, I found conditions unspeakable in the way of robbery. I arrested eight and turned them over to the patrol, but that is the last I ever saw of them or heard of them. I don't suppose they ever reached the jail."

Hurley says drays came later and moved the stolen articles away, despite the fact that the Boy Scouts, guarding the district, had strict orders to permit only Red Cross cars. It was the former policeman's opinion that members of

1921 Tulsa Race Riot "Angels of Mercy"

our race in self defence. However, he punctured his remark with an exception, naming those who came to the court house to avoid the proposed lynching of Dick Rowland.

The confession also involves a well known police official. He is Capt. George G. Blaine. Hurley stated that Blaine rode in one of the airplanes that hovered over the district during the riot.

1921 Tulsa Race Riot "Angels of Mercy"

Tulsa Tribune, June 5, 1921

ALL TRAINS OUT OF CITY JAMMED WITH REFUGEES

HUNDREDS OF NEGROES BUY ONE-WAY TICKETS OUT OF TULSA AGENTS SAY

A general exodus of negroes from the city has taken place since the rioting ceased Wednesday. All local passenger stations have been crowded with negroes buying one-way tickets out of the city. An approximate estimate was made last night that between 1,000 and 1,500 of them have left in the last three days.

They have been purchasing tickets for every city from New York to San Francisco at the Frisco and Santa Fe offices, railway officials announced. The Katy and Midland Valley offices have sold a large number of tickets for Muskogee and McAlester. Guthrie has also been a favorite among those who have decided to leave Tulsa.

More than five times as many negroes have left Tulsa in the last four days than at any other one period in the history of the city, the information clerk at the Frisco station said. However all of the negroes who left Tulsa did not leave by way of the railway stations as has been indicated by reports from surrounding towns of hundreds of blacks fleeing in all directions. The general exodus really began Tuesday night and became more spirited the faster the bullets flew Wednesday morning.

Last night when the last Midland Valley train left for Muskogee negroes were fairly hanging out of the windows. Cars reserved for negroes were jammed to the platforms.

1921 Tulsa Race Riot "Angels of Mercy"

Tulsa Tribune, June 5th, 1921

A troop of citizen deputies, every one having a record as a soldier or sure-shooting peace officer, has been snapped together in a close military organization which gives assurance that no disorder can last 30 minutes in Tulsa from this time on. Commanded by Lieut. Col. Patrick J. Hurley, and commissioned to act as an emergency police force by the Public Welfare Commission, this body of former Rough Riders, Spanish War veterans and plainsmen will be permanently on the qui vive and under orders for action in any crisis developing here.

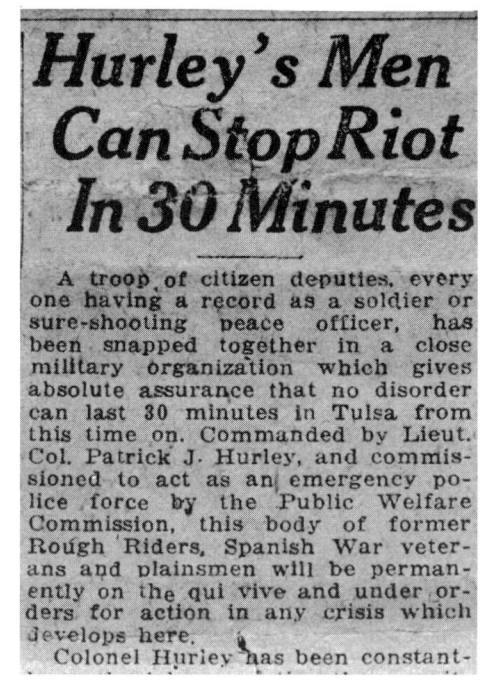

Colonel Hurley has been constantly on the job completing the recruiting of this company of mature and intrepid citizens for the last three days, and has been acting in conjunction with Sheriff McCullough, who has given each man a special commission in the county. Colonel Hurley was on the job last night at the sheriff's office, going through the details of his plan to deliver a telling blow to any outbreak before it could get fairly underway.

"I can say with assurance that no riot can break out here which will not be crushed before it ever gets started," said Colonel Hurley last night. "Every man on this force has his orders right now for any emergency that comes up . And we have the entire city covered. It will not be necessary to fire a shot, and the men in this company are not excitable men. They will quell the trouble quietly and quickly. Everyone of them is over 30 years old, and they all have service behind them as fearless men and straight shots. Within 10 minutes after excitement develops in any part of Tulsa, we will have a force on the job ample to smother it."

Judge Martin and nearly all the members of the Public Welfare Board were receiving reports until midnight on the situation around the city. Most left at that hour, after every rumor of disorder had been run down and found groundless. Mayor Evans & Commissioner Adkison sat with the board members and engaged in a general discussion of the problems confronting the city.

Jack Dillon, American Legion patrol in the Maple Ridge district, reported at the police station about midnight that he was on duty near Twentieth street and Owasso ave. at 9:30 p.m. when several shots, all appearing to come from the same place, were fired at him out of the darkness. Dillon said he threw himself flat on the ground and was not injured.

Daley and other National Guard officers were to leave early this morning with the Tulsa guard units for Fort Sill, Okla., where several thousand infantry, artillery and machine gun units are gathering for a 2 weeks encampment. These men will be only a few hours ride from Tulsa. A sufficient detachment of the local guard will remain in Tulsa to meet local needs.

The Public Welfare Board is to meet at 10 o'clock this morning with the expectation of remaining in session nearly all day.

Tulsa Tribune, Sunday, June 5, 1921

THE END OF ARGONAUT DAYS

A NEW and better day dawns for Tulsa.

Better cities grew out of the ashes of the holocaust that devastated Chicago, San Francisco and Baltimore. Those were disasters that were unforeseen and unavoidable. But as such disasters brought that which is better, so do the disasters that rise like a slowly accumulated cyclone of prejudices and lawlessness, bring in their wake a new conscience and a citizenship that is determined to correct. It is the history of such disasters as that which Tulsa has experienced that that which is bad is made better. By such disasters wrongs are worked into right. To make RIGHT is Tulsa's heroic and righteous resolve today.

Tulsa has a spirit which, however much it may have been dormant, is keenly alive today. It will never again recede to the indifference it has known in the past.

Tulsa is the capital of an El Dorado. It boasts of its wealth. But Tulsa is better than a city of millionaires: it is a city of generally distributed wealth and has the highest per capita wealth of any city in the world. Tulsa is young. When this territory came into statehood fourteen years ago Tulsa was a village. Today it is an ambitious little metropolis of one hundred thousand people. While this is a rich agricultural country it is the mineral wealth that has given this city its remarkable growth and put it at least fifty years ahead. Men have come to Tulsa to make money. Today they see a new duty -- to make a good city. Tulsa today is just emerging from her Argonaut era. Heretofore the average Tulsan has been too busy with his own private affairs to invest his conscience in his citizenship. The result has been that law enforcement has been lax for years. Gambling and bootlegging and hi-jacking have gone on little molested. And some of the time protected by the police. This has developed a lawless element.

Lack of law enforcement has permitted a bad negro element to develop a disrespect both for county and city officials and a lack of fear of all officers of the law..

Only recently a group of public-spirited citizens protested against these traditional conditions and the office of the attorney general of the state has been making searching investigations into the lack of efficiency of the city and county officers.

The city administration investigated itself and found itself practically spotless.

"Niggertown" has been a cesspool of iniquity. There most of the criminal of the community, both white and black, found harbor. There crimes were plotted. There an uprising has long been in process of planning. There this disorder began. The bad elements among the negroes, long plotting and planning and collecting guns and ammunition, brought this upon Tulsa just as the winds gather into a cyclone and sweep upon a city. This bad element among the negroes must learn that this is not a city of, for and by their kind. NEVER.

The United States government has suggested that it will look into this Tulsa affair. It should -- for the city and county police have been a sad bunch of servants of Uncle Sam. The Constitution of the United States has never meant much to them. Any preacher could go out in this old "Niggertown" and buy all the booze he might have the money to pay for. Yet the police didn't know of any place where it could be had. The police have been a disgrace on this whole subject of bootlegging -- a DISGRACE.

The bad element, white and black, must learn that there is a police power in Tulsa that will not tolerate lawlessness of any kind. Tulsa must have a police head that knows what his men are NOT doing. And Tulsa must have a police force that can and that WILL arrest the lawless and teach them that this is not a lawless town.

Moreover, Tulsa county must have a sheriff that does not go to bed when gunmen are collecting. Tulsa county must have officers who compel respect for the law.

The fair name of Tulsa cannot be redeemed by merely restoring the destroyed property. It must redeem itself before the world by establishing a reputation of being a city of law enforcement. For years it has had a national reputation for lawlessness and that must end NOW.

It is the old story -- a negro puts hand upon a white girl. The girl screams. The negro is caught and put in jail. The word is passed among the element that has not been taught to respect the law that there is to be a "necktie party" that night. That element of whites began to collect around the county court house and jail. It was largely a curious, good natured crowd. Then a small band of armed negroes came by auto to the scene.

The crowd was asked to go home. The police commissioner has since stated that he knew for some time past that the bad negroes had been at work in the negro quarter stirring up the negroes against the whites and that weekly meetings have been held over there. He says that some time ago he went over and talked with some of their leaders and told them that they would be held responsible if anything happened. All very nice as far as it goes.

The whites who gathered around the court house Tuesday night went away to get arms when they found the negroes arriving with arms. The negroes went away for more men and more guns. Before midnight "the war of races" was on in the streets of Tulsa and was carried into "Niggertown," where it raged until well into afternoon the next day.

The lawless whites went into

Frisco tracks where fight is said to have started.

"Niggertown" to "smoke 'em out" of certain places where the tough element congregated. This lawless element fought back the fire department. Then it started to loot the negro huts and houses. By Wednesday night "Niggertown" was a vast acreage of ashes and the state militia held the city under martial law.

It was a war of races, and racial prejudices are as old as history. They are not confined to southern cities. Chicago and Omaha, East St. Louis and Springfield, Illinois, and Washington, the nation's capital, have recently had their disgraceful stories. These stories are inevitable as long as young black men are allowed to grow up in a lawless atmosphere -- so long as police powers allow crime and disrespect for law to thrive unarrested.

As for looting, the shameless looting carried on in "Niggertown" is not alone a Tulsa story. Staid Boston experienced that. When her police failed her the lawless of Boston went wild in the game of loot. That sort of thing will always happen when the police fail. That which happened in Tulsa is likely to happen anywhere where racial prejudices are permitted to gain ground under a slow, smouldering fire and where the police force, through accumulative years of either corruption or incompetency, fail to cope with crime conditions.

But with that splendid spirit which is characteristic of the aggressively progressive Tulsan, Tulsa lifts her head from her hour of shame with a firm resolve to clean house and

Tents amidst the rubble.

to have a police force that can and WILL police the city. Tulsa has resolved that the crime carnival ends here and will be buried with the ashes of the "Niggertown" that is gone.

What is more, the public spirited, prideful citizens of Tulsa have met in conference to resolve and lay plans to rebuild and restore that which the lawless have destroyed and to build a cleaner, a better and a more sanitary section of the city than that which ends in ashes.

Tulsa will redeem her splendid name before the world. The Argonaut days of Tulsa are history. The finer city with a nobler and truer spirit and an awakened conscience is the aftermath of this disaster.

Tulsa Tribune, June 5, 1921

PRISON FOR RIOT CHIEFS, JURY ORDER

Judge Biddison to Demand Action

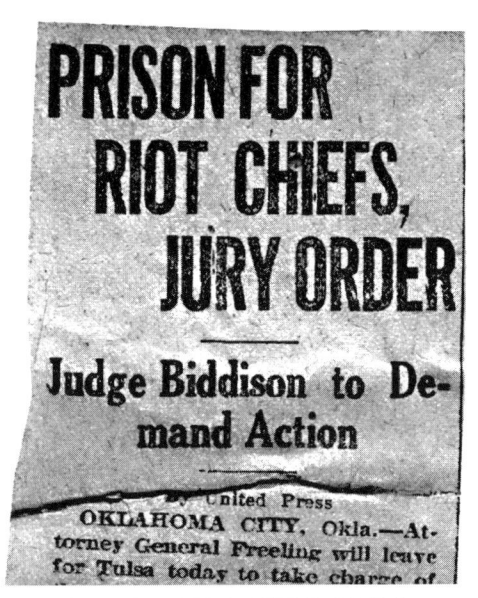

United Press

OKLAHOMA CITY, OKLA. -- Attorney General Freeling will leave for Tulsa today to take charge of the grand jury investigation of the race riot there, it was announced here last night.

Regarding the investigation, Freeling said: "I am going into this matter to find out in every manner possible where the blame for the terrible crime belongs, and if the grand jury does not appear to mean business, I will establish a court of my own." Freeling and Governor Robertson held a long conference yesterday over the coming probe when the grand jury convenes Wednesday.

"My instructions to the grand jury when it convenes Wednesday will be to leave it's whitewash brush at home, "was the answer of District Judge Valjean Biddison when asked last night if the forthcoming grand jury investigation into the Tulsa race riot called by him at the direction of Governor Robertson is to be a real inquiry which will achieve definite resolution.

"You may say to the people of Tulsa," declared Judge Biddison, "that I shall instruct the grand jury to make a comprehensive inquiry into every phase of the race riot, the causes, both direct and indirect, which may have lead up to it, and everything that followed as a consequence of that startling catastrophe. I shall recommend prison bars for those who have committed felonies.

"I shall tell the grand jury in plain and unmistakable language to return true bills against all persons of whatever station or color, guilty of rioting, murder, arson, robbery, looting or dereliction of official duty, let the chips fall where they may."

After making it plain that the investigation, so far as it lies within his power, will be for the purpose of punishing or removing from office any person found guilty of crime or malfeasance or non-feasance in office, Judge Biddison explained that his powers are circumscribed and only directory at best.

To Scan List Closely

"I have nothing to do with the selecting of the men who will compose the grand jury," said the judge, " except that I can reject any taxpayer I do not think fitted for grand jury service after he has been summoned in the regular way. Neither have I anything to do with the final findings the grand jury makes. I can only instruct it as to what I believe it should investigate then the matter passes entirely into it's hands.

"I see no reason why a whitewash should be anticipated," Judge Biddison continued. "So far as I can determine, public sentiment is practically unanimous in its demand that this thing should be sifted to the very bottom for the purpose of disclosing the causes that led to the riot and the true facts in connection with it."

In accordance with Judge Biddison's statement covering some of the specific matters which will be considered, his formal instructions, to be presented to the grand jury when it convenes Wednesday, may be expected to take up the following matters.

FIRST: The remote causes which may have brought on or tended to have brought on the riot. These, it is generally thought will include:

Phases To Be Covered

A query as to whether there has been a laxity of law enforcement in the immediate past, on the part of either city or county officials, which may have brought about conditions of which the race riot was the natural result. This may include charges that "dope" peddling and indiscriminate intermingling of whites and blacks in the negro district have flourished alarmingly.

An investigation of the persistent rumor that there has existed in the negro section a secret organization for the purpose of inciting racial feeling and compelling racial equality, which has been fostered by regular meetings and inflammatory articles in the local colored press. Police Commissioner Adkison has already stated since the riot that the police have long known of a secret organization of some kind there.

Further probing into the declaration of the attorney general's office and the statement of citizens that there have been dance halls in the negro district where the whites and blacks have danced and drank together undisturbed almost nightly for many months past.

A searching inquiry into the reported alarming growth of the drug and "jake" habit among the negroes, the result such condition might have on them if it exists and the statement of prominent negroes that the band of armed blacks which marched to the court house and participated in the battle there was nearly altogether composed of drug fiends and liquor users.

Downtown Invasion

SECOND: The direct cause or causes of the riot, which may include:

An inquiry as to whether the negroes invaded the downtown district with guns believing one of their race was to be lynched and attempting to save him, or only made this an excuse for an outbreak which had long been brewing.

A query as to whether there really was any attempt being made or about to be made to lynch the negro prisoner, Dick Rowland, and if there was, what brought it about.

An investigation of the claims of some of the negroes that someone telephoned for them to come uptown armed and the assertions of members of their own race that they were organizing and storing ammunition at the Tulsa Star office some time in advance and sent runners throughout the negro district to summon certain men sometime before the trip to the court house.

THIRD: What took place during the riot, including the acts that were unlawful, uncalled for & are deserving of punishment.

Judge Biddison said every phase of the riot would be included in his sweeping instructions and he expected the grand jury to leave nothing unconsidered which should be taken up.

He said he would call to the attention of the grand jury the invasion of the downtown district by the armed negroes, the gun battles that took place, the breaking open of stores and taking guns therefrom by the whites, the burning of the negro district, the reported shooting down of innocent parties, the vandalism that took place in the devastated area, the conduct of all those in authority just before and during the rioting and other things which took place or are reported to have taken place.

"It may be that some of these acts were excusable; it may be that others merit imprisonment for the guilty parties," said Judge Biddison. "That is not for me to determine. I shall only call these reported facts to the attention of the grand jury and recommend that they probe them fully, returning recommendations which will mean trial in the criminal courts or removal from office if warranted in any case and exonerating the accused from blame where they are found to be blameless or their acts justified."

The veniremen summoned will assemble at the court house Wednesday morning at 9 o'clock. It probably will be Thursday before the grand jury is empaneled, sworn in and ready to begin the taking of testimony. It is expected to remain in session several weeks. Attorney General Freeling will come to Tulsa Sunday and will have complete charge of the grand jury's work.

How Jury is Drawn

The jury will be composed of 12 men. It is selected in the following manner: In the office of the clerk of the courts, Mrs. Frances H. Harvey, is a box containing the names of all Tulsa county taxpayers eligible to jury service written on slips of paper.

Mrs. Harvey, or an assistant, reaches into the box at random and draws 24 names one at a time.

These names will be given to Sheriff William McCullough and he will summon the 24 men to appear for grand jury service Wednesday. Their names are placed in another box. They are drawn out one at a time. When 12 men thus drawn qualify, they constitute the grand jury. Judge Biddison may reject any of the men called for sufficient reason. If the grand jury is bad it will either be because the average of Tulsa county citizenship is that way or because fate has played a scurvy trick with law enforcement in their chance selection.

Rubble on both sides of train tracks.

1921 Tulsa Race Riot "Angels of Mercy"

Tulsa Tribune, Sunday, June 5, 1921

PRESS SCOLDS TULSA; EDITORS BLAME POLICE

CITY'S SPIRIT IN PROMPTLY AIDING NEGRO SUFFERERS PRAISED

The Tulsa race riot and incendiarism of Tuesday and Wednesday has attracted editorial attention from many of the country's leading newspapers. Throughout nearly all the comment there runs the opinion that an adequate police department could have averted the trouble. Following are some of the excerpts gleaned from The Tribune's exchanges.

Recommends Greenville's Plan

St. Louis Times: Tulsa, the miracle city, whose growth has astonished the world, has won a less enviable distinction by having a race war. As usual, it had small beginnings. A negro boy, charged with insulting a white elevator girl, was arrested and locked up in jail. There was no earthly probability of his escaping punishment.

But some white hoodlums spread the report that the negro was to be taken from jail and lynched, for which report there was no basis. Some negro hoodlums appeared immediately afterwards and a fight began which turned into a small war and resulted not only in the death and injury of many whites and blacks, but in the destruction of many homes.

Perhaps this dark page in the city's history is due largely to surprise, to failure to guard against such an uprising.

The history of Greenville, Mississippi, may be of value to Tulsa and to other cities where both races reside. In Greenville there has been a working agreement between the best white citizens and the best negro citizens. If a negro commits a crime, the best negro citizens catch him and turn him over to the authorities. If the white hoodlums begin a fight on the negroes, the best white citizens take charge of the hoodlums and see that they are punished. Under this arrangement Greenville has long been practically free from race friction. Criminals are criminals and law is law.

Efficient Police Chief Need

Kansas City Star— The rioting at Tulsa, with its tragic outcome, is another reminder of how insecure are the bases of civilization when once they began to topple. People think of order as solidly established as a permanent aspect of American life. Then the are awakened by sudden outbursts of fierce race clashes in East St. Louis, Washington, Omaha, Chicago and now in Tulsa.

In no instance was there provocation looking to such a disastrous outcome. But the inflammable material was present.The torch was applied , authorities failed to extinguish the fire at the outset, and the flames spread until they were out of control. In Tulsa, as in the other cities cited, unoffending men and women, the bulk of them black, were shot, their homes burned and untold misery inflicted, simply because the lawless elements in the community got out of hand.

The people of Tulsa are no different from the people of other cities. Under similar circumstances the same thing might occur in a hundred places, The only safety lies in prevention, in suppressing any disorder before it gets underway. That in turn depends on an efficient police force.

There has been no case of race rioting which could not have been stamped out by prompt and intelligent police action at the outset. A city that permits its police force to become the spoils of politics is risking a deluge of such misery as has just visited Tulsa.

An efficient police force is essential to maintaining civilized standards in American cities.

Will the Problem Remain?

Louisville Courier-Journal--- "My prescription is silence and slow time." said Dr. Edwin Anderson Alderman, president of the University of Virginia, in discussing the race problem in southern states.

Vividly these words of this man of light and leading in American life come to mind as right-thinking Americans soberly reflect upon the depressing intelligence from the city of Tulsa, Okla.

Law there has been defied. Constituted authority has been scouted. Property has been ruthlessly destroyed. Human life has been wantonly snuffed out.

Indignation will be expressed and recorded. Explanations will be made. Causes will be not assigned. Danger signals will be hoisted. Warnings will be issued. Crimination and recrimination will be interchanged.

When all this is done with, the subject will be not greatly affected. The patient will be anaesthetized. The malady will remain uncured.

Very seriously may be asked the question: Is there soon to be a solution of the problem presented by incidents in American life like that at Tulsa?

Grover Cleveland saw things as they are. He had courage of high order—the courage that refuses to blink a fact.

"I think I see the solution of almost every problem that confronts our people," said this bravely sincere man a few years before his death. "Plutocracy will be checked. Warfare between capital and labor will cease. Other questions will be discussed, compromised and settled. But there is one problem in American life for which I foresee no solution. It is the race problem---the negro question."

Tulsa is the industrial metropolis of Oklahoma. Its negro population is large including the vicious "cross" between the negro and Creek Indian. The combination is not a happy one. There as elsewhere the negro has become the victim of the dangerous propaganda that the negro needs to go around to escape injustice. He was armed at Tulsa. The result is now known.

Tulsa's Mob Bath.

Topeka Capital: Tulsa appears to have come out of its fit of mob rule more quickly and with a clearer sense of disgrace than is ordinarily the case in a debauch of race hatred. Possibly national prohibition may have some relation to this quick recovery of sanity.

"Tulsa," the chamber of commerce through its president announces to an on-looking world, "feels intensely humiliated, and standing in the shadow of this great tragedy, pledges its every effort to wiping out the stain at the earliest possible moment and to punishing those guilty of bringing the disgrace and disaster to this city."

It is unfortunate for a city to obtain fame for such orgies or savage rioting as convulsed Tulsa for two days. They do not pay.

If Tulsa is prompt in fulfilling the promise made by her chamber of commerce she will come out of the most unfortunate episode in her history with less discredit than many cities. Yet repentance and restitution are not a cure of the evil of race violence in the United States and of mob rule. Prevention is the only true remedy, and this is a hard problem in education.

Fruits of Mobocracy

Doubtless the first of that train of causes which culminated in an orgy of murder, incendiarism and vandalism at Tulsa, probably the most horrifying mob-crime ever committed in this country, is to be found in a spirit of insolence and lust among a few negroes which inevitably arouses and makes resentful the white race's consciousness of superiority, as well as its determination to maintain that superiority and the integrity of its blood.

But once we advance from this incipient cause, we but accumulate evidence that the guilt for that frightful crime attaches itself mostly to the white race.

It is the fruit of mobocracy, a harvest true to the sowing. That is the fact to be imprinted indelibly upon the mind. It is indeed the only one which there were any profit in emphasizing. The temptation to dilate on the significance of the indictment which that crime brings against our civilization and of the shame which the spectacle at Tulsa casts upon the residents of that city is strong. But one could indulge in it to no practical end. One whose intelligence and impulses do not make him immediately sensible of those consequences will not be made so by preachments. And, in fact such a use of the subject would only touch the superficial details of it.

In its extent and certain incidents the tragedy at Tulsa is distinctive. But it is merely characteristic in relation to its causes. The spirit which begot it is not peculiar to Tulsa, nor to Oklahoma. It is pervasive, and particularly so in southern states, the honest commentator must acknowledge, however, reluctantly.

Cost Must Be Figured

Wichita Eagle--- As the excitement dies down and the smoke clears away, Tulsa begins to realize that its day of madness must be followed by a morning of repentance and mourning. In a generation Tulsa will not wipe away the stain.

Then there is the bill to pay. Taxpayers must pay for the folly of the mad mob. Tulsa is wondering today what that bill will amount to.

It is better to pay a little every year for insurance against mob violence. A good police department, well organized by experienced men, well drilled for mass action, well armed for emergencies, is an expensive adjunct of a city government, but no city can afford to be without such a department. It seems quite likely that a flying squad of well-armed, well-drilled policemen could have broken up the Tulsa mob during its inception. A police department must have semi-military training and right organization to be able to cope with such situations. A good police reserve squad, armed with shotguns and trained to handle disorder without losing temper, is the best insurance against rioting. New York has a riot whenever anybody gets excited, but five minutes after the first squad of reserves arrives the riot is over.

Coupled with police protection, there should be in every city a well-defined policy, well known to all citizens, of bringing all offenders against women and girls to swift retributive justice through the working of the courts. Such crimes should be punishable by life imprisonment---nothing less. Then it should be a matter of pride with the courts and prosecutors to see that offenders of this sort are sent up promptly and mercilessly. The community that permits official trifling with such cases is drawing down upon itself the retribution of mob violence as surely as daylight follows night.

Thinks Agitators to Blame

Fort Worth Star-Telegram: No good citizen will seek to minimize in any degree the enormity of the race riot at Tulsa, Okla. It was an outrageous and disgraceful affair. Judged merely on the surface it is almost beyond belief that such a thing could happen in a civilized community.

However, it is very necessary that it should not be judged merely on the surface. It is time to face certain facts and to speak plainly about them. Violence of the furious and vehement character of the riot at Tulsa does not "just happen." Tinder must be lying about for the spark to ignite.

What was the underlying cause of the Tulsa riot? As much as any citizen, white or black, may deplore the affair, it is necessary to ask that question.

The evident intent at an unspeakable crime by a negro upon a white girl does not explain the whole of the affair. Such crimes stir white men to the very depths of their being, and properly so. It is the protective instinct of the race, which is primal and fundamental. But even this does not explain entirely the affair at Tulsa. There must have been something else.

An examination of the details of the incident will disclose that there was something else. Consider the circumstances.

A crowd of negroes marched to the court house, according to the dispatches, apparently for the purpose of liberating the accused negro.

But even yet that does not explain the riot. Why would a crowd of negroes gather around the courthouse in such circumstances? Anyone in his senses must have known beforehand what such a demonstration would lead to. To speak plainly those negroes were inflamed by a violent propaganda against the whites which negro radicals in Chicago, New York and other points in the East have been carrying on since the armistice.

Publications filled with denunciation of the white people of the South and with lurid descriptions of imaginary wrongs of the negro race have been spread throughout the South during the past two years and a half. The most extreme of them have preached violence, if not openly, covertly and by innuendo.

The Tulsa riot is a direct result of the sullen and ugly discontent which these Eastern propagandists have been planting on the breasts of Southern negroes. It is among the "frst fruits" of their teachings. The homeless negroes of Tulsa who view the ruins of the results of their labor and who witnessed their relatives being killed in a furious riot, are the victims of this propaganda. That is the plain truth and there is no sense in seeking to close your eyes to it.

And we must face the whole truth. This propaganda must be dealt with. It constitutes a problem of the South, which not only the white people but the best leaders of the negroes in the South must face. The Tulsa riot was an outrage. But the real instigators of it were these agitators. To fail to recognize this would miss the solemn lesson which the whole ghastly business carries with it.

Blames Law Officers

More blame for the shame of Tulsa should be attached to the officers of the law than to the members of the mobs. People are much alike everywhere and when Tulsa depends for law enforcement on men of the caliber she has in office now, you can expect the lawless element to run wild. Tulsa has reverted to Indian Territory type and throughout the world today people who know or care anything about Oklahoma, are saying, "Well, what could you expect? That never will be a law abiding community."---Bartlesville Enterprise

Menace of Race Friction

The need of earnest effort to discourage race friction is very clear. Neither the government nor leaders of public opinion can afford to condone it under any condition.. The nation the state and the community should realize that the danger is ever present at this time, and preparedness should be the watchword of those in authority. The sheriff who prevents mob violence is a better officer than he who merely disperses a mob after its passion has burned out.--St.Joseph News-Press

1921 Tulsa Race Riot *"Angels of Mercy"*

Tulsa Tribune, June 6, 1921

VANDAL SUSPECTS TO BE TURNED TO COUNTY OFFICERS

MEN AND WOMEN ARE HELD FOR STEALING

Thirty men and women arrested for vandalism in the wake of the two-day race riot will be turned over to county officials for prosecution on charges of larceny, according to A.C. Sinclair, assistant city attorney. The suspects are now held in the city jail, but police authorities expected that they would be turned over to the county officials late this afternoon.

Police this morning estimated the value of stolen goods they have recovered at $10,000. The storeroom in the basement of the jail is jammed with recovered property, little of which has been identified.

Many Mexicans visited the jail this morning and identified some of the property as stolen from them.

Tulsa Tribune June 6, 1921

WHITES HELD FOR STEALING AUTOS IN BURNED AREA

Two more white men were lodged in the county jail today to face charges in connection with alleged looting in the negro district during the riot. They are B.W. Wallace, charged with auto theft and C.T. Parr, held for highway robbery.

Wallace was in the negro district trying to sell a Hudson super-six. Negroes he approached knew a car of that description had been stolen from Charley Scott, 1431 S. Carolina., negro, during the riot and told him Scott might buy the car. Scott claimed to be anxious to purchase and lured Wallace to the Hudson garage where he telephoned police.

On further information given by Wallace the car was found 51 mile from Tulsa, near Okmulgee, where it had been abandoned with a broken axle. Scott identified it as his property.

Jake Mayes, a negro taxi-cabdriver, claims that Parr held him up while he and his wife were fleeing from Tulsa in a Ford wednesday morning and compelled them at the point of a gun, to abandon the car. Parr then drove away in the car Mayes claimed.

1921 Tulsa Race Riot "Angels of Mercy"

Tulsa Tribune, Monday, June 6, 1921

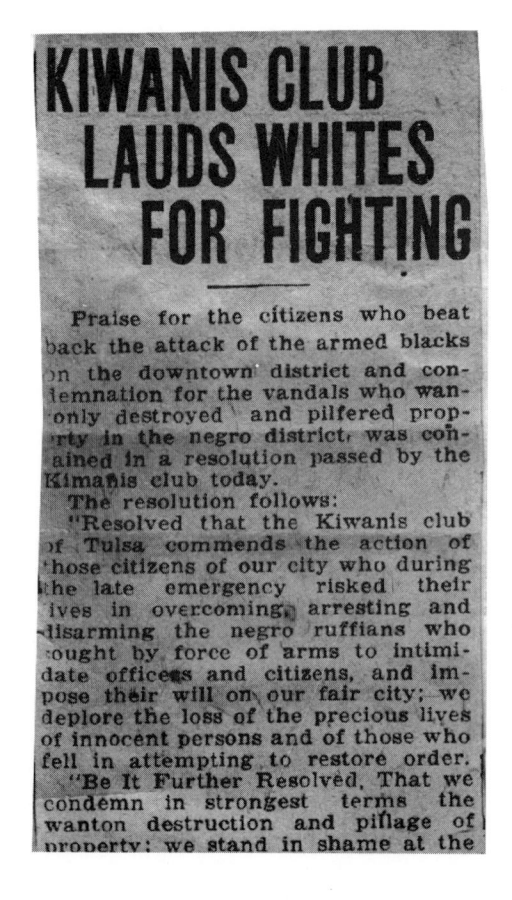

KIWANIS CLUB LAUDS WHITES FOR FIGHTING

Carload of armed whites.

Praise for the citizens who beat back the attack of the armed blacks on the downtown district and condemnation for the vandals who wantonly destroyed and pilfered property in the negro district, was contained in a resolution passed by the Kimanis club today.

The resolution follows:

"Resolved that the Kiwanis club of Tulsa commends the action of those citizens of our city who during the late emergency risked their lives in overcoming, arresting and disarming the negro ruffians who sought by force of arms to intimidate officers and citizens, and impose their will on our fair city; we deplore the loss of the precious lives of innocent persons and of those who fell in attempting to restore order.

"Be It Further Resolved, That we condemn in strongest terms the wanton destruction and pillage of property; we stand in shame at the acts of these vandals and pledge our every assistance to the authorities in bringing each of them to speedy justice.

"Be it Further Resolved, that we express our confidence in the Executive Committee of Board of Public Welfare and pledge it our support and assistance."

60

1921 Tulsa Race Riot *"Angels of Mercy"*

Blacks Flock to Marriage Bureau, Make New Record

Cupid is sitting perched on the smoking ruins of the negro district with arrow drawn. He may be a black cupid---but he is Cupid just the same.

He was discovered down there by Hal Turner, marriage license clerk at the court house, who says he issued 23 marriage licenses Saturday, nearly all to negroes. The run on the hymeneal altar was continuing unabated today.

Turner attributes the remarkable increase in the number of licenses issued to negro couples to the fact that many girls who have heretofore refused to say "yes" when they had good homes of their own and were living in comfort have accepted the protection of their dusky suitors since the burning of the district has forced them to face the future penniless and without a roof to cover their heads.

And if the bride needs a new hat?

Or a new dress?

1921 Tulsa Race Riot "Angels of Mercy"

Tulsa Tribune, Monday, June 6, 1921

Once more today the black robed sisters of the Holy Family Catholic school, 820 S. Boulder av., are quietly saying their masses and going silently about their duties in the shadow of the great church after three days of unwonted tumult in their lives spent in ministering to the homeless negroes who crowded the school to its doors.

About 3 o'clock Wednesday afternoon the first of the refugees began to arrive and 400 had assembled at the Holy Family school before night fell. The St. Vincent De Paul ladies' organization of the church combined forces with the sisters and cared for them until 5 p.m. Friday, when the last had been removed to their homes or central headquarters.

Among the 400 who arrived on the opening day were 25 babies. These were bathed and re-clothed. The adults were furnished with food and clean clothing where necessary, the Knights of Columbus buying them out of their private fund. Meals were served to 250 Wednesday, 150 Thursday and 75 Friday.

The ladies of St. Vincent De Paul's are planning a meeting this week when they will offer their services as a body to assist in the permanent relief and reconstruction work to be carried on by the citizenship of Tulsa.

Thinks Our Escutcheon Is Tarred

It will be years and years before the good people of Tulsa will be able to wipe away the stain, to eradicate the blot which the rioting of the past twenty-four hours has placed upon its fair name and smeared across its escutcheon. For years and years which will come with unborn Time, the name and fame of Tulsa will suffer from this blackening event---Ardmore Ardmoreite.

Really, Jerry, This Is Not Clubby

Whenever the Magic City goes in for anything, it goes every other city one better. Just wait for the Chamber of Commerce to insert an advertisement in the metropolitan papers reading like this: Business openings---Tulsa wants factories; Tulsa wants jobbing houses; A splendid opening here now for a wholesale undertaking establishment.---- Okmulgee News.

Report of a Medical Committee meeting:

> June 6, 1921.
>
> Report from Medical Committee.
>
> Report on Financial matters. Arranged that Fields, Terrell and Avery should arrange handling of funds and distribution of funds.

Matter of feeding taken up. Decided all dependents should go to fair grounds and all mass feeding done there. Reported that arrangements had been made at Booker Washington school to feed all workmen over there for 15 cents per meal and deduct it from wages.

Graham suggested getting all superfluous people out of white residence section, and issuing permanent passes to and from the fair grounds to responsible working people and daily passes to others. Question of jitney service to and from fair grounds for working people, and question of supplies for semi-permanent camp taken up.

Kates moved that Graham and Maj. Fuller be instructed to confer with Executive Committee, with full power on the part of Graham and Fuller to act with the Executive Committee to get all excess people out of servants' quarters and move them to the fair grounds- to act with Central Committee and Mr. Terrell.

Mr. Fields asked Kates to include motion to feed refugees and issue passes.

Kates moved to give Graham and Fuller complete authority to work out any scheme that is advisable to them and the Executive Committee and police identifying refugees by card, keeping off streets, moving, etc.

Willows stated that was not a matter which should be settled by Red Cross themselves, and whatever action is taken should be taken conjointly, in order that a united front might be presented to the people.

Kates stated that motion included recommendation for jitney service and everything else.

Willows stated that this would be placed in the hands of these men, to report back tonight.

Motion seconded, and upon vote unanimously accepted.

Question of setting up stands and stores taken up. Chief Police stated Hopkins was handling that.

(Continues on next page.)

Mr. Fields: At first we had a clear understanding that the regular funds of the Tulsa Chapter were nor to be put with this relief fund, as St. Louis informed us that their manner of handling relief funds is to handle it as separate from Chapter funds until all other resources are exhausted and then, if necessary, use our Chapter funds and then go back on St. Louis.

Mr. Willows: Our understanding with the Committee was, get your bills together and when you need money to pay them, bring them to us.

Question of employment taken. Decided to consolidate with all other employment agencies and it was suggested that Chairman of State Federal Agency be Chairman of such committee. Mr. Ireland to handle this matter as he sees fit.

Question of payroll taken up. Anyone who is to be paid out of Red Cross Funds to report to Murray or Willows.

Kates brought up question of fire protection at fair grounds and Police Chief said they were attending to it.

Fields stated he would like Central Committee put on record as requesting them to feed workmen.

Murray reported that Borden is going to put on an inventory man and going to take an inventory of all Red Cross stuff.

Willows asked police to take action on matter of supplying transportation for negroes backwards and forwards over and around town, and to take action to stop this transportation by whites.

Registration Room, numbers identify; 1. Dawson, 2. Scott, 3. McCartney, 4. Abbott

Tulsa Tribune, June 7, 1921

Two More Negroes Dead, Boosts Total Death Toll to 34

Another name was added to the list of Negro dead this morning when Howard Barrens, 19, died at the Cinnabar hospital at 2 o'clock from the effects of a gunshot wound he received beneath the heart. The body will be sent to friends in Catenville, Tex., for burial.

This brings the negro death list up to 24. Ten whites are known to have been killed. Yesterday afternoon an unidentified negro was found two miles north of Dawson near the Curtis flying field, shot through the neck. Efforts to identify the body were futile. It was taken to the Stanley-McCune morgue.

BOARD PLANS NORMALCY IN RULE OF CITY
Soon to Give Reins to Commission Again

A plan of gradual transfer of the detailed responsibilities of the Public Welfare Board back into the hands of the city commissioners and other local officials, with the retention by the board of the supervision and policy-directing functions of reconstruction and relief, was outlined by Judge L.J. Martin, chairman of the board, in a statement this morning to the press and members of the board.

The first steps in this transfer would involve the work of policing the city and handling the clean-up in the burned area, and Judge Martin proposed to the board before its adjournment this noon that Commissioner Steiner be empowered to take over the force of men employed to establish order in the black belt.

1921 Tulsa Race Riot "Angels of Mercy"

Tulsa Tribune, June 7, 1921

NOTICE

Beginning Wednesday morning, June 8th, the police will arrest ALL NEGROES who appear on the streets without proper identification.

In order to permit negroes who are peaceful and working in permanent jobs free use of the streets there will be provided a green identification card WHICH MUST BE SIGNED BY THE EMPLOYER AS A MATTER OF IDENTIFICATION.

It will, therefore, be necessary for employers to come with their negro help to the City Hall, Police Station, Red Cross Heights, Booker Washington school, or the Free Fair Grounds and identify them before Wednesday morning if same are expected to appear on the streets of Tulsa on or after Wednesday morning.

NEGROES WHO ARE NOT SUPPLIED WITH IDENTIFICATION CARDS WILL BE ARRESTED AND TAKEN TO THE FAIR GROUNDS FOR PERMANENT IDENTIFICATION BEGINNING WEDNESDAY MORNING

J.M. ADKISON,
commissioner of Police.

1921 Tulsa Race Riot *"Angels of Mercy"*

Tulsa Tribune, June 7, 1921

TULSA STILL TARGET FOR EDITORS' IRE

CONCEDE, HOWEVER, THAT SUCH DISTURBANCES ARE NOT CONFINED TO TULSA

Newspaper editors of the country, particularly of the east, where they are more ignorant of conditions in the southwest, continue to lambast the city of Tulsa for permitting the race disturbance here last Tuesday and Wednesday. Following are extracts from more of the leading papers:

Tulsa's Race Riot

Chicago News:

There was a repetition of the old story in the Tulsa race riot. A crime by a vicious negro, rumors of a lynching, preparations to resist it, a collision between a few rough and lawless armed whites and a few blacks of the same type-- and mob psychology did the rest.

The result is shocking--a hundred or more dead, heavy property losses, thousands rendered homeless and destitute.

The reports indicate that if the Tulsa police and other authorities had exercised ordinary prudence and foresight the riot might have been averted entirely or reduced to small proportions. The negligence, weariness and inefficiency of the local authorities permitted the armed toughs of the town to take command of the situation.

Fortunately the governor of Oklahoma and the military force ordered by him into Tulsa are now....*(The newspaper clipping ends here.)*

1921 Tulsa Race Riot   *"Angels of Mercy"*

68

1921 Tulsa Race Riot *"Angels of Mercy"*

Tulsa Tribune, June 7, 1921

Virtue is bold, and goodness never fearful.
Shakespeare, Measure for Measure.

POSITIVE POWER

ONE thing is proven: Tulsa can be well policed and well governed. The Committee on Public Welfare today governs Tulsa. There are strong men in this city, men who have courage as well as character, men who have positive force as well as personal honesty, men who are generals and not guileless, men who have the capacity to see a job before them and seeing, DO IT; men who do not have to seek the forlorn hope of hiding behind the thinnest veil of a smoke screen. Tulsa has men who can govern Tulsa and make Tulsa a fine city. Such men are the Committee of Public Welfare. The city is in good hands. Let's keep it in good hands until we work out some of the plans that will carry us permanently into a good government and into that efficiency which will build a Tulsa that we will be proud of wherever we go, and not a Tulsa for which we feel disposed to apologize because of its crime reputation.

    NOW is the time to work out the plans for a managerial form of government.

    NOW is the time to put into operation a council of social agencies.

    The conscience of Tulsa is at last awake. There are big things ahead of us. Negative goodness does not make a city administration strong; it takes positive goodness to do positive things. Tulsa has had a positive job with a negative power at the helm. If we are to realize a bigger and better future, we must have a positive administration to build it.

1921 Tulsa Race Riot *"Angels of Mercy"*

Scene during Tulsa Race Riot June 1st 1921

Tulsa Tribune, June 7, 1921

POLICE ORDER IDLE BLACKS TO FAIR CAMP

"WORK OR QUIT WHITE DISTRICT." EDICT IS ISSUED

Temporary relief work among the homeless negroes who were victims of the race riot last week has assumed the aspect of army routine in the last two or three days with the negroes doing practically all of the work under the supervision of Red Cross directors.

Only 400 negro women and children and a few men remained in the fairgrounds camp today of the 5,000 or 6,000 who were taken care of there last Wednesday night and Thursday. However, with the issuance of a police order yesterday by commissioner J.M. Adkison that all servants quarters in the white district must be vacated by negroes not working, at least 1,000 negroes are expected at the fairgrounds by tonight.

The police order, also issued yesterday, which requires all negroes to wear green identification tags, probably will help augment the camp at the fairgrounds as it will force idle negroes who have no employers to obtain these tags for them to either go to the camp on their own accord or be taken there by police.

Negroes Do the Work

With the connecting up of gas plates in the main building at the fairgrounds most of the negro women are doing their own cooking. The kitchen, which is still maintained, is in charge of Danny Craigo with Miss Helen Black acting as assistant. They direct the work of cooking food for the sick women and children.

Negro women do the cooking and the cleaning is done by the negro men who still remain t the camp. Practically all of these men are the heads of families that are being cared for there until the men can find work and provide a place for their families to live.

Mrs. Harriett Wardell is in charge of the nursing and first aid quarters where the mothers and sick children are taken care of. Here also the negro nurses are doing practically all of the work. During the day several women from the Red Cross headquarters go to the camp to assist Mrs. Wardell in supervising the work.

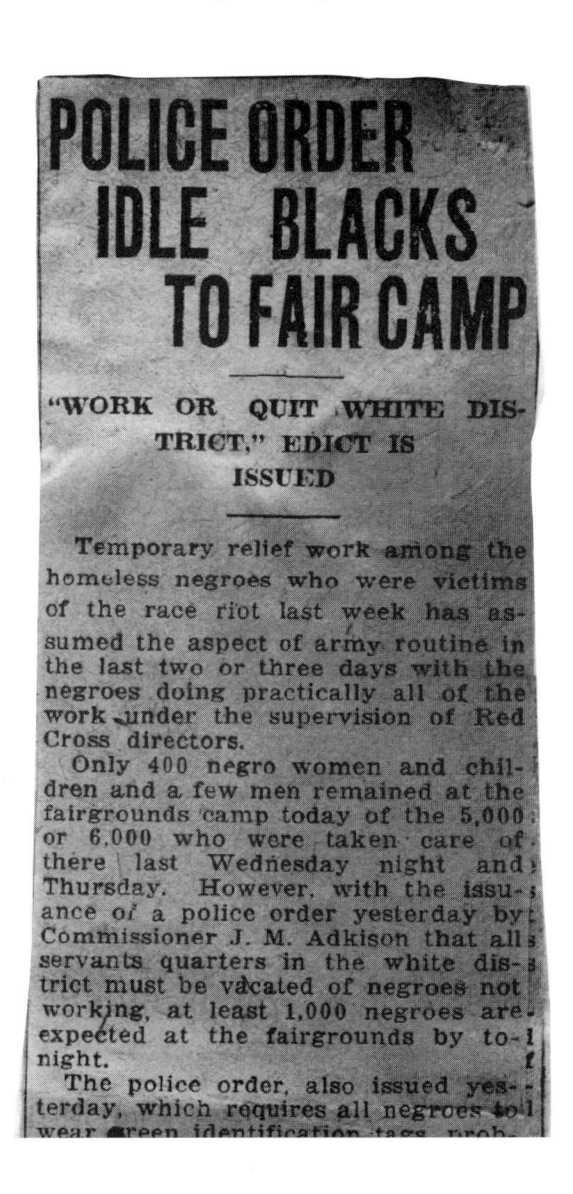

Tulsa Tribune, June 7, 1921

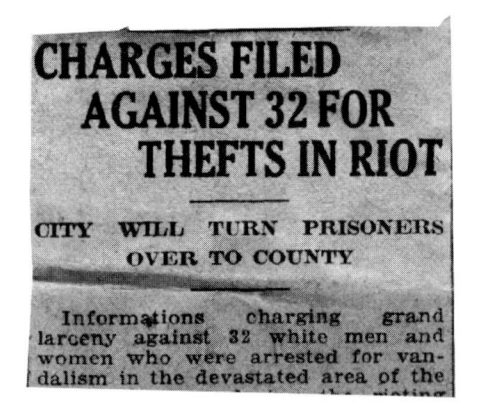

CHARGES FILED AGAINST 32 FOR THEFTS IN RIOT

CITY WILL TURN PRISONERS OVER TO COUNTY

Information charging grand larceny against 32 white men and women who were arrested for vandalism in the devastated area of the negro quarters during the rioting last week were issued by the county attorney this morning. seventeen of the accused are now in the county jail and will be transferred to the county authorities this afternoon.

Those who are now in the custody of police are: C.A. Olson 319 East Thirteenth Place, charged with theft of a victrola, belonging to C.J. Jefferson, 823 East First Street.

Ray Hemtrick, 1216 East Admiral Blvd, charged with the theft of a Winchester pump-gun belonging to the Barden Loan Co.

Bunch, first name not known, living at 534 S. Xanthus Ave., is charged with theft of two silver vases valued at $75 and a lamp shade valued at $25 from H.O. Abbott.

E.J. Tutter, West Tulsa, is alleged to have stolen six rugs, clothing and bed linens, belonging to H.D. Abbott. Another charge against Tutter alleges that he he stole a valuable ring belonging to H.D. Abbott, also

T.L. Murphree and Ruth McNair are jointly charged with looting the home of Ida Gilmore, 417 N. Detroit ave. of a perculator,, umbrella, knitted cap, a brown fur, silk shirts, blankets and other wearing apparel.

W. Gill and V.E. Van English, 213 N. Frisco ave. are alleged to have stolen seven sheets, a red serge dress, blue gingham dress, four percale dresses, two blue and voile dresses and other articles from a home in the devastated area.

Walter Thorpe, 1806 W. Brady ave., charged with theft of a trunk and its contents belonging to W. Scott and valued at $25.

H. Forkner, 401 N. Cincinnati ave., C.H. Gregory, 16 E. Easton ave., Ella Freymouth, 310 S. Lansing ave., C.L. Deavser, 331 S. Yorktown ave., and Louis Jacobs, E. First St., are others whom charges were filed against for the theft of various articles.

PRESS PRAISED BY ARMY HEAD FOR PEACE AID

BARRETT EXPRESSES THANKS TO CITIZENSHIP FOR HELP IN RESTORING ORDER

Tribune, June 4th, 1921

Before leaving the city last night after lifting the martial law ban Adjutant General Charles F. Barrett took occasion to praise the press of Tulsa and the citizenship for the support given him in helping to restore law and order.

"I hold the newspapers of Tulsa in high esteem and cannot compliment them too highly for the part they played in assisting us to restore order and carry on the reconstruction work here," said the military commander.

The adjutant general said a statement that he had used the words a "reporter for a yellow journal" with reference to the riot had been misinterpreted. He said he had not meant to infer that articles printed in local papers had contributed to the riot.

Tulsa Tribune, June 8th, 1921

FEDERAL LABOR BUREAU TO DEAL JOBS TO BLACKS

ALL AGENCIES COMBINE TO HANDLE EMPLOYMENT

An agreement was reached by the allied employment agencies of Tulsa yesterday whereby the federal employment office, under manager E.N. Ellis, at 14 1/2 E First st., is to become a clearing house for whites and negroes seeking employment during the reorganization period.

Persons wishing to employ either white or negro labor for any purpose, under the agreement, are asked to leave their names and addresses with Mr. Ellis. He will then notify the particular agency able to furnish the help wanted. Both whites and blacks seeking employment may also leave their names at his office.

The meeting was participated in by representatives of the white Y.W. and Y.M.C.A., and the colored Y.W. and Y.M.C.A., organized labor and other organizations. A second meeting is to be held today at which hopes are held out of patching up the differences between Tulsa contractors and the union workmen.

Negro women looking for employment will be cared for at present by a secretary at Mr. Ellis' office. The negro Y.M.C.A. has headquarters in a tent near the Booker Washington school and negro men out of work can either call there or at the federal employment office, 14 1/2 E. First st.

A committee on employment was named as follows: Federal employment bureau, E.N. Ellis; white Y.W.C.A., Mrs. Victor A, Hurt; white Y.M.C.A., Miss Elsie Williams; Allied labor unions, Ben James; Colored Y.M.C.A., G.A. Gregg; joint Y.W.C.A., Mrs. Biles.

The negro Y.W.C.A. hostess house will be put in operation today at Archer and Cincinnati when a secretary of their own race will also look after the colored women seeking employment there. The white Y.W.C.A. has issued a request for furniture to equip these quarters and donations of second-hand furniture of all kinds will be welcomed.

Charles Page helped the situation materially when he promised to house, free of charge, 150 negro women who are employed and give them free transportation to and from Tulsa on the Sand Springs railway.

Tulsa Tribune, June 8th, 1921

COOKE

While we are speaking of preachers, we'd like to say that among others Rev. Harold Cooke has stood out as a mighty good and useful citizen. He has the aggressive honesty. He is not a mere guileless gentleman; he has the qualities of a general. He wouldn't be bad timber for Mayor. This is not a nomination. This is not an announcement of our choice. It is a commendation of Harold Cooke---good citizen. It is a declaration that we need more citizens of his caliber and his kind.

GET A GREEN CARD

The green card system is a good innovation at this time; as with every other class and kind of people, there are good negroes, bad negroes and indifferent negroes. As always it is the bad who bring misfortune on the good. The bad negro is not helping the cause of his people in any community when he tries mob rule with gun in hand. The city does just what it should do when it gets rid of the negro who cannot give a good account of both his time and conduct.

The green card does something more than to help the city get rid of a bad negro. It is the certificate of industry and decency to every negro who carries it. It marks him as of the better class, just as the absence of the card brands the other fellow as one to be looked upon with suspicion if not to be rid of. In this hour of reconstruction in our city let every good negro who is entitled to his green card, get it without delay.

1921 Tulsa Race Riot *"Angels of Mercy"*

Card replicas courtesy of the Tulsa Historical Society

IDENTIFICATION CARD

Name _____

Sex _____ Age _____

Permit for Passage _____

_____

_____

_____

NOTICE——This card expires at dark on this date. Police are to arrest bearer unless he is in Fair Grounds or_____ quarters before dark of this date.

Date_____

Signed --

Copy of "Green Card" referred to in preceding page.

✚ **Headquarters American Red Cross** ✚
= TULSA, OKLAHOMA =

JUNE_____, 1921

_____

IS AUTHORIZED TO **PASS** ALL GUARD LINES AND MILITARY PATROLS, ON RELIEF DUTY.

Countersigned by   **CLARK FIELDS,**
Byron Kirkpatrick,   *Chairman.*
Major, Adj. Gen. Dept.

ANY GROCERY

Please furnish Groceries to the amount of
ONE DOLLAR
to bearer and charge to the American Red Cross.

CLARK FIELD, Chairman.

THIS IS YOUR REQUISITION.

Copies of original cards issued by the Red Cross.

1921 Tulsa Race Riot *"Angels of Mercy"*

Tulsa Tribune, June 8th, 1921

Thousands of Green Tags are Issued to Negroes With Jobs

There are not many negroes in Tulsa minus jobs.

That is the conclusion reached by city officials following the city hall tag day yesterday. Officials did not know today how many thousands of tags were issued to negroes who have steady employment. They do know that 7,500 were printed and this supply was exhausted.

Because there were not enough of the green tags for the working blacks, officials this morning suspended the order that all negroes not wearing the green tag would be arrested. This order will not be put into effect until tomorrow morning it was announced.

The city hall was jammed yesterday by negroes seeking tags. Another packed house this afternoon was anticipated when tags from a fresh supply will be distributed.

Sees No Moral Lesson

There is nothing in the insensate outburst at Tulsa from which to draw the usual "moral lessons." Prejudice and rancor were, of course, at the bottom of it, but the animating motive was corn whiskey in bad Creek negroes who spoiled for trouble. Both the whites and blacks of Tulsa are equally to blame, however, and the officials chosen to uphold the law are deserving of the severest condemnation.-----

Guthrie Leader

1921 Tulsa Race Riot *"Angels of Mercy"*

Card replicas courtesy of the Tulsa Historical Society

AMERICAN RED CROSS

Refugee Card

R. R. TRANSPORTATION

To _____

CITY TRANSPORTATION

To _____

EMPLOYED

At _____

SHELTERED

At _____

BED AND BEDDING

_____

MEDICAL AID

At _____

By _____

PROVISIONS ISSUED

June

CLOTHING FURNISHED

POLICE PROTECTION

AMERICAN RED CROSS

CLARK FIELD, Chairman

NAME_____

ADDRESS_____

Approved_____

Front and back replica of Red Cross Refugee Card.

Tulsa Tribune, June 8th, 1921

2 BOND SUITS FILED AGAINST NEGRO EDITOR
CONTINUE HUNT FOR A.J. SMITHERMAN

A.J. Smitherman, negro editor of the Tulsa Star, for whom a warrant has been issued as a result of last week's race trouble, was made defendant today in two suits to collect bonds, filed by County Attorney W.A. Seaver.

The county attorney alleges that A.J. Smitherman and Will Davis made bond for Ed Doyle and David Enoch charged with selling liquor in the old negro district, in the sum of $500 each, that the trial day has passed and neither the defendants nor the bondsmen can be found.

Although a search is being made for Smitherman in all parts of the county in connection with the riot charge, no trace of him has been found. It is charged by other negroes that the negroes gathered at his printing office prior to their armed invasion of the uptown district. His brother, J.H. Smitherman, a former deputy sheriff is in jail.

John Stratford, held in jail in Independence, Kansas, charged with being one of the riot leaders, continues to fight extradition to Tulsa for trial. It is expected that the extradition papers will be presented to Governor Robertson for approval today and go immediately to Governor Allen at Topeka.

1921 Tulsa Race Riot *"Angels of Mercy"*

79

1921 Tulsa Race Riot   *"Angels of Mercy"*

Tulsa Tribune, June 8th, 1921

Corporation To Re-Build Homes, Plan

A housing corporation with capital sufficient to finance the building of homes on a large scale and on a non-commercial basis, is one of the proposals now pending before the Public Welfare Board as a means of rapid reconstruction in the burned area.. Judge L.J. Martin, chairman of the board, advocated the organization of such a corporation yesterday as a channel of affording employment to many idle negroes and an opportunity for men of means here to unite in a constructive manner for rebuilding devastated homes.

The building of small homes on the financing of a housing concern was urged by Judge Martin as a matter of civic progress in a general way, and it was his proposal that the corporation loan the funds for wage-earning white men as well as negroes to build their own homes. The proposition was put forward by Judge Martin outside of any final plans formed by the Welfare Board to cover losses incurred by property owners in the burned area. Further consideration was to be given the matter at a meeting of the board today.

"The housing corporation plan has become most successful in many cities where it has been worked out," declared Judge Martin , "I have a letter from a big concern in Chicago backed by the biggest business men in Chicago, which offers to give us co-operation at service at the present time in building homes on a large scale. Some means of united effort is necessary, and I believe this offers the best solution for quick work."

1921 Tulsa Race Riot *"Angels of Mercy"*

Progress report on Committees:

> REPORT OF MEETING HELD IN THE PRIVATE DINING ROOM OF THE Y. M. C. A. CAFETERIA JUNE 8, 1921.
>
> After luncheon the meeting was opened by Mr. Maurice Willows in the Chair. Mr. Willows spoke in a general way of the progress made by the various Committees and Sub-Committees.

REPORT OF MEETING HELD IN THE PRIVATE DINING ROOM OF THE Y.M.C.A. CAFETERIA JUNE 8, 1921

After luncheon the meeting was opened by Mr. Maurice Willows in the Chair. Mr. Willows spoke in a general way of the progress made by the various Committees and Sub-Committees.

Miss Rosalind Mackay, of the Medical Department, reported that all patients under medical care will be removed from the Fair Grounds, hospitals, etc., into the hospital which is to be established in the Booker T. Washington school. Four rooms in the unit back of the main school building will be used for this purpose. Plumbing, carpentering, furnishing, etc., of these rooms will be under the direct supervision of Dr. Reeder and Miss Mackay.

Miss Mackay reported there are 32 patients now in the Emergency Hospital. These will be moved into the new hospital when ready.

Miss Mackay will have a report of all expenses in her Department, nurses' salaries, supplies, hospital bills, etc., ready for the meeting to be held tomorrow, June 9. Beginning tomorrow the nurses will be placed on a monthly basis of approximately $150 per month and expenses.

It was decided to employ two Negro Doctors to be on duty (one in the day time and one at night) at all times. These doctors will take care of patients at the Fair Grounds and other temporary quarters. The hours and salary to be paid will be decided by Dr. Reeder and Miss Mackay.

It was reported that the kitchen at the Emergency Hospital was furnished by the Community Kitchen, without expense to the Red Cross.

It was decided to proceed in purchasing as many more tents as the Committee deems necessary to temporarily house the refugees in family groups.

Tent for temporary family housing.

Mr. Borden reported the Accounting Department has their books opened. An approximate report of purchases made to date, excluding Wednesday and Thursday, the first two days of relief work, amounts to $20,000. Invoices on about half of these purchases have been received and will be paid as soon as possible.

Red Cross Purchasing and Accounting office.

Dr. Fields reported the Central Committee requests that we have published daily a list of subscribers to the relief fund.

Mr. Lewis Lefko, who is in charge of the Claims Department, reported that this work is now underway and a record is being made of the claims of those refugees who lost property by fire or loot. These records are made for future reference only and no promise is being made those who file these records that they will ever be recompensated for their losses. Mr. Lefko reports that the claims are usually very much over-estimated, but are being carefully checked.

Mr. Harry Heinzman called attention to the great importance of maintaining the morale of the Negroes and plans for this work will be presented at the meeting to be held tomorrow noon.

The meeting adjourned at 1:15.

M. B. Adams,

1921 Tulsa Race Riot "Angels of Mercy"

Tulsa Tribune editorial, Saturday, July 23, 1921
(This story refers to Police Chief John Gustafson & Police/Fire Commissioner J.M. Adkison)

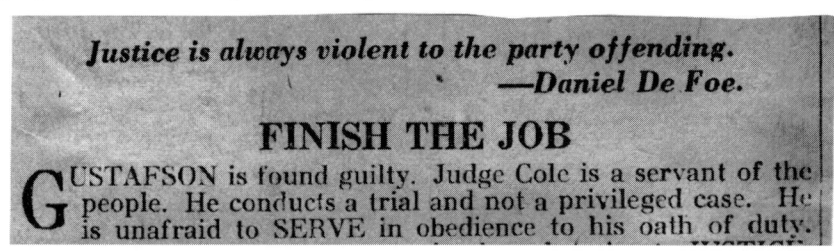

> *Justice is always violent to the party offending.*
> —Daniel De Foe.
>
> **FINISH THE JOB**
>
> GUSTAFSON is found guilty. Judge Cole is a servant of the people. He conducts a trial and not a privileged case. He is unafraid to SERVE in obedience to his oath of duty.

GUSTAFSON is found guilty. Judge Cole is a servant of the people. He conducts a trial and not a privileged case. He is unafraid to SERVE in obedience to his oath of duty. The jury deliberated with a conscientious devotion to JUSTICE. All honor to judge and jury. Tulsa is beginning to have some real honest respect for law and order, but it comes not through the city administration but in spite of it.

The city administration has been considerably off the job of late that it could be AT the trial. Mayor Evans has repeatedly made the statement that the trial was a farce. The statement was a boomerang that came home. The verdict proves that it was not the trial that was a farce, but the city administration. The city administration was all devotion to the indicted Chief.. It was not thinking half so much about the people as it was the Chief. It forgot that it was not elected to protect an indicted Chief but to protect a too poorly protected people. ??????????????????????????attended to the people's business and their own.

City Attorney Duncan was not far wrong when he said the city administration itself was on trial. But we would not want to go so far as to say that the city administration itself is found GUILTY. Rather it may be said with a greater measure of truth it has been found guileless. This is no time for a guileless crew at the head of our city government.

When Meachem, on the stand, said that he beat up a preacher (that is the stamp of too much of our police activity, beat up and intimidate the decent citizens and let the crooks glide by), when, to repeat, he said he beat up a preacher he guffawed,--everybody laughed. The courtroom was filled with the "everybody" that was there to help Gustafson--the Mayor laughed. Yes indeed that was some joke, that beating up of a preacher. A merry joke. Quite amusing to everybody, BUT THE JURY. The jury did not laugh. The jury saw the infamy of it all, The jury brought in the verdict which The World characteristically said many spectators believed to be a miscarriage of justice. The spectators which The World quotes were naturally friends of Gustafson. They filled the courtroom.

When Adkison was on the stand he had to admit that there were no books kept by Gustafson which would show what moneys were taken in, there was no check.. These are sidelights on the police administration that came in with the great reform ticket that was going to clean up and do the town some long needed good.

Mayor Evans, that great crusader for righteousness, has said that it was all politics. Guileless again. It has not been a political battle. He who sees nothing but a political battle in it is too blind to be about without some child hand to guide him. It has been a battle for decency and decency has won. That is all there is to it. The community's thanks to the judge and the jury.

If the city administration has hopes of rebuilding public confidence it can make no better start than to ask for Adkison's resignation.

Tulsa Tribune, Sunday, July 24, 1921

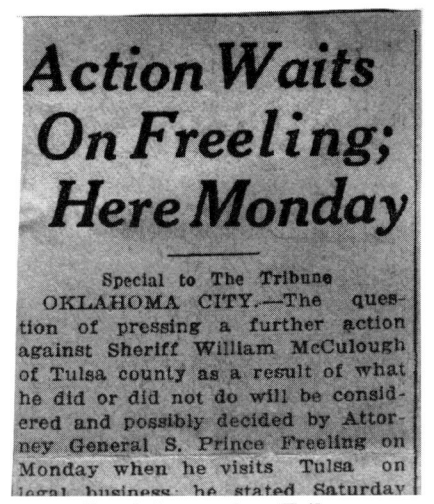

Action Waits On Freeling; Here Monday

Special to the Tribune

OKLAHOMA CITY----The question of pressing a further action against Sheriff William McCullough of Tulsa county as a result of what he did or did not do will be considered and possibly decided by Attorney General S. Prince Freeling on Monday when he visits Tulsa on legal business, he stated Saturday night. Little consideration had been given the matter of McCullough's position in the short time since the Gustafson verdict was announced, Mr. Freeling said.

Declaring that the conviction and removal of former Chief of Police by the unanimous jury verdict here Friday night will have a far-reaching effect not only in Oklahoma but all over the country, the attorney general expressed his official satisfaction that the law had been upheld and mob violence struck a heavy blow.

"I consider this a very valuable verdict," said Mr. Freeling. "It will have a far-reaching effect in the state and outside the state, wherever this spirit of mob violence has gained a foothold. That verdict teaches that an aroused citizenship will finally demand from elected officers that they enforce the law and protect the community."

Glad Law is Upheld

"I emphasized in my opening statement to the jury that the riot matter was of paramount importance," continued the attorney general, "We brought out the evidence on that point fairly and without exaggeration and the jury gave a unanimous decision. I feel no sense of personal satisfaction in the verdict, nor do I have any personal feeling against Gustafson. I am proud, however, that the law of the state has been upheld and that Tulsa has led the way in showing officers of the law that they cannot turn a city over to a mob and hold their positions."

The attorney general expects to make an address before a Sunday school gathering in Miami today.

Mrs. Kathryn Van Leuven, assistant attorney general, who has shouldered the burden of gathering evidence on law enforcement conditions in Tulsa and later in directing the trial of Gustafson after Mr. Freeling was called away, termed the verdict of the jury: "A great victory for the citizenship of Tulsa."

Appeal Will Fail

'This is the first time in the history of the state that a citizenship has by a jury verdict brought to the bar of Justice an officer who has failed to do his duty in a riot crisis," said Mrs. Van Leuven. "The verdict was right, and I am confident that if the appeal is taken to the supreme court the jury decision will be upheld. An appeal is really purposeless, however, in view of the fact Gustafson and those city officials who held him in office will long since have completed their terms before the appeal reaches the supreme court."

Mrs. Van Leuven stated that she was tired out after her strenuous work of the past few weeks and said she might enjoy a few days of well earned rest at home.

Tulsa Tribune, September 14, 1921

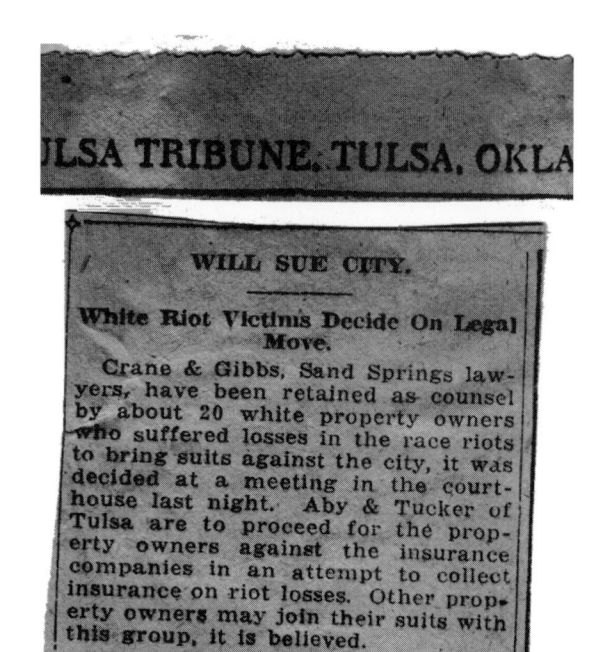

WILL SUE CITY
White Riot Victims Decide On Legal Move.

Crane & Gibbs, Sand Springs lawyers have been retained as council by about 20 white property owners who suffered losses in the race riots to bring suits against the city, it was decided at a meeting in the court house last night. Aby & Tucker of Tulsa are to proceed for the property owners against the insurance companies in an attempt to collect insurance on riot losses. Other property owners may join their suits with this group, it is believed.

CONTINUE RIOT CASES

During the sounding of the criminal docket Wednesday by District Judge Redmond S. Cole, the cases against six Tulsa negroes charged with participating and inciting the race riot were continued by agreement. The case against Dick Rowland, negro, charged with assault, was dismissed. It was Rowland's alleged attack on a white elevator girl that led to the race disturbance on the night of May 31st. His dismissal followed the receipt of a letter by the county attorney from the girl in which she stated that she did not wish to prosecute the case.

The case against J.R. McElhaney, charged with passing a bogus check, was dismissed by the court when the county attorney showed the defendant had died subsequent to the commission of the alleged offense.

Trial of Henry Canard, charged with murder, was continued for the term because of the absence from the state of several witnesses.

Clipping from Tulsa Tribune, date unknown.

YOU TELL 'EM
Every Day a Tribune Reporter Asks a Question of Five Persons Whom He Selects at Randam.

TODAY'S QUERY

What do you think of the proposal to create a new negro district, reserving the south part of the burned area for a wholesale and industrial center?

Clarke Whiteside, realtor--- Of course I am strongly favor of it. Because the property there is much more valuable to the city as industrial blocks than as a residential section. For consideration of the city's and the residents' best interests no frame buildings should be rebuilt there. I hope that general support will be accorded to the plan to make it a section brick and stone buildings.

Mrs. G.O. Hollow, 815 E. Nineteenth st.--- The idea is wonderful. . That low ground is suited for business purposes. And the colored people can have a far more beautiful and desirable residential place by moving farther out. If the plan is well managed and deliberately formed, it ought to succeed.

T.J. Hartman, president Producers State Bank---I believe it is a splendid proposition for the negroes and the city at large. The negroes if moved farther north would be better situated unquestionably. The devastated area would be made the center of a huge industrial and wholesale center. And in doing this it is certain that the property would be increased in value to the benefit of the negroes. This money would enable them to build better homes in a district farther removed from the heart of the city.

E.Roger Kemp, president Sinclair Oil & Gas Co.---That would be a good move for all concerned providing it is properly handled. It must be seen to that the negroes have their interests absolutely protected and get the increase in the value of the property if this is done.

Miss Bertie Coffey, stenographer Cosden building---I think that is the proper thing to do. The black district is now too close to the heart of the city to avert serious trouble in the future. But the negroes should be given the full value of their property and have their new quarters laid out for them with a view to sanitation and architectural beauty.

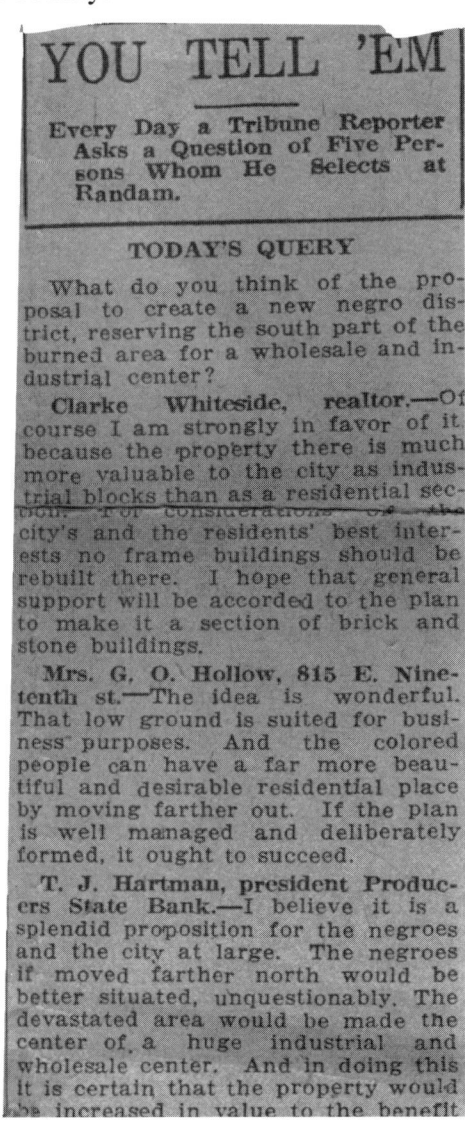

1921 Tulsa Race Riot *"Angels of Mercy"*

This newspaper clipping from Mr. Willows' collection has no heading and no indication of date or newspaper. It is included here because it obviously refers to the "recent riot". The first part of the article is missing.

long years of law and order to wash away the stain which Tulsa put upon her own character by the murderous riots of Tuesday night and Wednesday. The city cannot clear itself on the ground that the trouble was merely the sudden outbreak of a disorderly minority. The police power exists specifically for the purpose of protecting the public against possible offenses of such criminal minorities as are known to exist in every community of any considerable number.

With the majesty of the law on their side, police officials of character and resolution can prevent any such orgies of arson and murder as Tulsa has just presented. But the fault cannot be loaded entirely upon the craven cowardice and inefficiency..........if it was not criminal complicity........... of the city authorities. These men were the duly chosen representatives of the entire voting population of the city. If their morally criminal failure to do their duty in a crisis cannot be charged to any such intent on the part of the electorate, it is still true that the result proves Tulsa voters guilty of a very serious lapse in the exercise of their power of intelligent selection. Tulsa knew that the very makeup of her population rendered such an outburst possible, and it was entirely in her power to know whether the men whom she was electing had or had not the character to meet such a situation. We are not alleging that Tulsa is a sinner above many other cities. It is not many months since Columbus was wakened at midnight by the alarm signal, calling troops into readiness to send into a neighboring Ohio city, disgraced by arson and murder as the same character as that of Tulsa, and less only in extent. And in Ohio as in Oklahoma, ordinary courage in the performance of sworn duty would have prevented disgrace from which the community must suffer in reputation for years to come.

(Story continues on next page.)

Not a Sectional Matter

Louisville Courier Journal-"Insofar as Oklahoma is of the south, the south must share her shame," is an editorial comment concerning the Tulsa riot.

Shall Americans fresh from participation in the world's greatest war and at a moment when even the president of the United States is deprecating the faintest manifestation of sectionalism and bidding his countrymen to think and feel and act in terms of the blood-baptized national spirit, persist in this miserable parochialism that insists at every opportunity upon stressing some "sectional" angle or striking some discordant "sectional" note?

To the last degree, this habit is childish.

Riots have nothing whatsoever to do with geography. Lawlessness is not a matter of latitude or longitude. Tulsa's shame, misfortune, or whatever it may be characterized, is no more the responsibility of Mississippi than it is of Maine, no more that of Virginia than it is of Vermont.

Why lug in "the south?" What has "the south" to do with lawlessness in Oklahoma that every section of the country has not?

Within the last 20 years race riots have broken out in Atlanta, New Orleans, Elaine, Arkansas; Chicago, Omaha, East St. Louis, Springfield, Illinois; Washington, D.C.; Springfield, Ohio; Wilmington, Delaware, and Independence, Kansas. In each case the race rioting was between whites and blacks.

Run through this list of towns. Note the geographical situation of each. How many of these are in "the south" and how many are not in "the south?"

The American commonwealths that lie in the more southern portion of the United States have doubtless the defects of their qualities, precisely as other commonwealths situated elsewhere have. These qualities and these defects are throughout America to be found approximately equal in degree and identical in character. America is one nation, and one nation in spite of every attempt that may be made to chop it up into sections and to split it into rival groups.

Also America is one people. If Appomattox settled one thing it settled that question, or should have settled it. If it failed to settle it, surely San Juan Hill, Santiago, Manila, the Marne, the Alsne, Chateau Thierry and the 80,000 American heroes -- not "southern," or "eastern," or "western," or "northern" -- but "American" heroes who sleep in France--should have settled it.

Throughout the earth wherever the American flag floats---the flag of the United States of America, not the flag of "the north," or of "the south," or of "the west," or of "the east," but the flag of the United States of America---it floats "at half mast" today in honor of the memory of a great American, a great patriot, who happened to be born in the state of Louisiana. By accident of birth, education and environment he was, 50-odd years ago, a Confederate soldier. Since 1865 he was denied the high privilege of being a "southerner" and accorded the yet higher privilege of being an American.

East, west, north, south, and even unto the insular possessions, every man, woman or child under the protection of the American flag has but one country, in which worthy citizens know no section and glory in their single nationality.

Tulsa's shame, Oklahoma's shame, is America's shame, precisely as Oklahoma's honor or Tulsa's honor is America's honor.

1921 Tulsa Race Riot   *"Angels of Mercy"*

90

1921 Tulsa Race Riot "Angels of Mercy"

The Oklahoma Sun, December, 1921

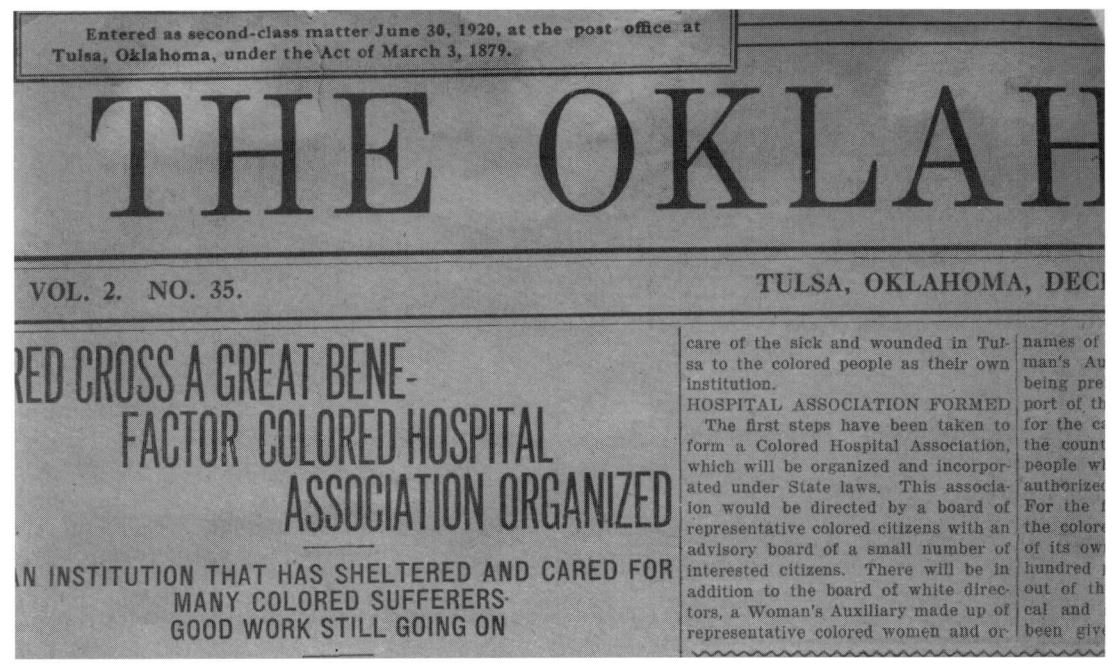

THE OKLAH[OMA SUN]

Entered as second-class matter June 30, 1920, at the post office at Tulsa, Oklahoma, under the Act of March 3, 1879.

VOL. 2. NO. 35. TULSA, OKLAHOMA, DEC[EMBER]

RED CROSS A GREAT BENEFACTOR COLORED HOSPITAL ASSOCIATION ORGANIZED

AN INSTITUTION THAT HAS SHELTERED AND CARED FOR MANY COLORED SUFFERERS- GOOD WORK STILL GOING ON

care of the sick and wounded in Tulsa to the colored people as their own institution.

HOSPITAL ASSOCIATION FORMED

The first steps have been taken to form a Colored Hospital Association, which will be organized and incorporated under State laws. This association would be directed by a board of representative colored citizens with an advisory board of a small number of interested citizens. There will be in addition to the board of white directors, a Woman's Auxiliary made up of representative colored women and or[ganized]...

The old saying, "Tis an ill wind that blows no one good" is coming true. The colored population of Tulsa will always remember with gratitude and thanksgiving the fact that nothing has been left undone by the Red Cross to heal the wounds of the sick and maimed following the June riot. The best surgical, medical and nursing care has been provided every riot sufferer and no expense has been spared in caring for the sick whose homes were burned and where home provisions for caring for sick people were limited.

When it became necessary for the Red cross to vacate the hospital at the Booker T. Washington school, the colored people were quick to respond to a suggestion made by the Red Cross that a new hospital be erected on a cooperative plan whereby the Red Cross would furnish all the material necessary for a hospital building if the colored people, thru Central Relief Committee, would furnish the labor.

With surprising swiftness, a thirty-bed hospital was built and equipped with every essential for scientific surgical care and treatment of the sick. The hospital building is located at 324 North Hartford on the site of the old Dunbar school.

It has one large surgical ward for men, a surgical ward for women, a maternity ward a general medical woman's ward, dining room, kitchen, bath, linen closets, and best of all a thoroughly modern operating room, fully equipped. A large porch running the full length of the building on the east provides ample space for convalescent

1921 Tulsa Race Riot "Angels of Mercy"

patients during the sunshiny days, and a like porch on the south side answers the same purpose during the chilly days. Two convalescent tents have been equipped for ambulatory patients. Likewise a tent for tuberculars is provided on the grounds.

Up to the present time, the Red Cross has conducted this hospital as a riot relief proposition. It has served its purpose so well that the institution has become indispensable. It has been the desire of the Red Cross Committee, County Officials and Mr. Willows particularly, for the Red Cross to leave a permanent institution for the care of the sick and wounded in Tulsa to the colored people as their own institution.

HOSPITAL ASSOCIATION FORMED

The first steps have been taken to form a Colored hospital Association which will be organized and incorporated under State laws. This association would be directed by a board of representative colored citizens with an advisory board of a small number of interested citizens. There will be in addition to the board of white directors, a Woman's Auxiliary made up of representative colored women and organized in such fashion that every colored woman in the district can become identified with the movement. The title to the hospital building and equipment will be turned over to the Colored Hospital Assoc.

The hospital will be generally supervised by Dr. Butler, County Physician, (white) who will have to assist him a staff of colored physicians and surgeons whose services will rotate. Colored nurses will be employed by the Association, and in every sense of the word the institution will be their property, a thoroughly democratic institution, operated, owned and controlled by the colored citizens.

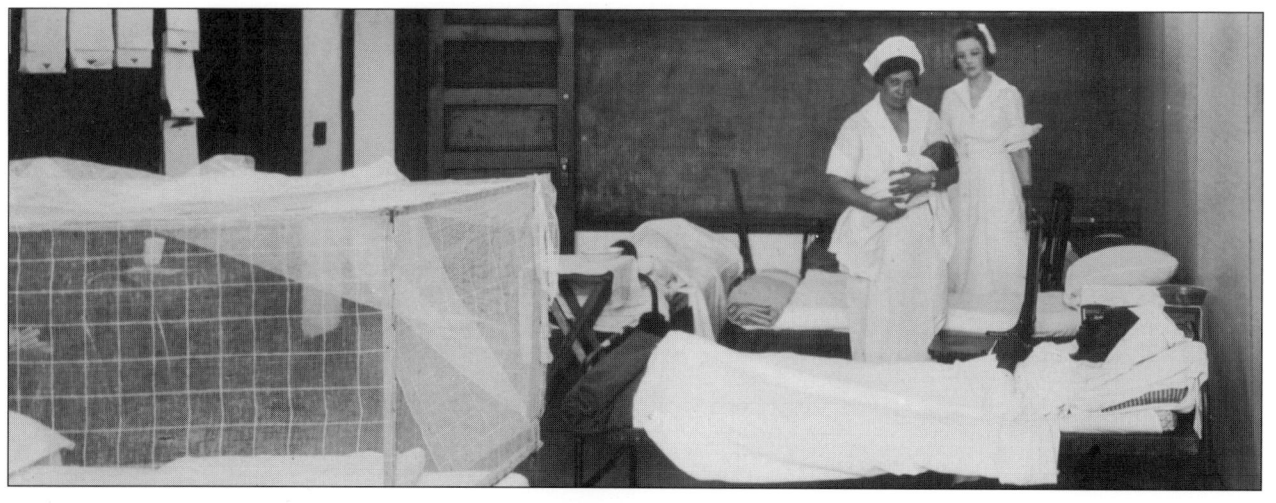

Nurse holding infant they called "June Riot."

1921 Tulsa Race Riot *"Angels of Mercy"*

1921 Tulsa Race Riot *"Angels of Mercy"*

This is the hand-written letter to Mr. Willows from a pastor and his wife expressing the gratitude of the negro people.

> Tulsa, Okla.
> July 1, 1921
>
> Mr. Maurice Willows,
> Red Cross Headquarters
> Tulsa, Okla.
>
> Kind Sir:—
>
> This comes to express to you the profound gratitude not only of every Negro in Tulsa but throout the civilized world where ever there is a Negro. Words fail me in trying to express our appreciation for your noble work for us. You and the "Great Red Cross" are helping us as a Race to shut out of our lives, all that is evil, to do our "Duty" and in that way we hope to receive the pure the beautiful, the good and true, and when the time comes that we shall add our motto to the music of the sphere it will be full of Joy & Thanks giving no harsh

1921 Tulsa Race Riot "Angels of Mercy"

This is page 2 of the handwritten letter to Mr. Willows. He quotes it in the opening of his official Red Cross report:

note to mar the full harmonious sound." "We have but faith we can not know; For service is of things we see and yet we trust it comes from Thee, a beam in Darkness let it grow." Knowing that God will reward you for what you have striven to do for us. For what you are doing. and for what you will do; in His words we read what is done for the least of His subjects is precious in His sight.

Is the prayer of a grateful people,

Very Respectfully yours
Lovella S. West
J. S. West Pastor of
A. M. E. Church

1921 Tulsa Race Riot   *"Angels of Mercy"*

96

1921 Tulsa Race Riot "Angels of Mercy"

Tribute to the Red Cross and Mr. Willows:

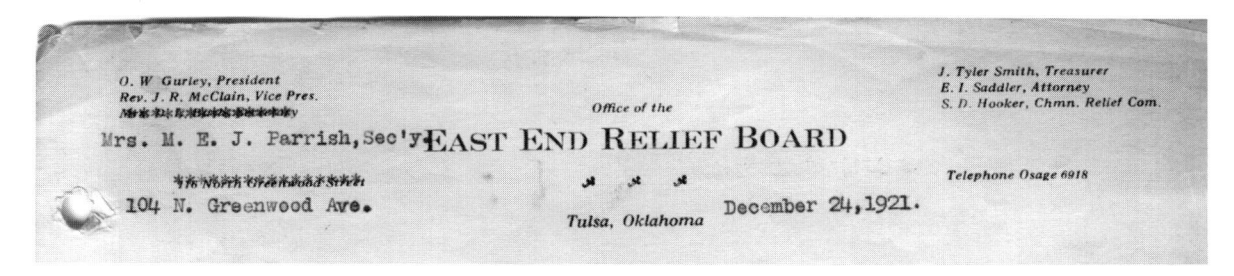

```
O. W. Gurley, President                                              J. Tyler Smith, Treasurer
Rev. J. R. McClain, Vice Pres.                                       E. I. Saddler, Attorney
                                   Office of the                     S. D. Hooker, Chmn. Relief Com.
Mrs. M. E. J. Parrish, Sec'y  EAST END RELIEF BOARD

                                                                     Telephone Osage 6918
104 N. Greenwood Ave.
                              Tulsa, Oklahoma     December 24, 1921.
```

The courage with which Tulsa Negroes withstood repeated attempts of the city administration to deliver the "burned area" over to certain land grafters is the subject of most favorable comment all over the country. The rapidity with which business buildings and residences are being built, in most instances, better than before is proof in wood and brick and in stone, of the black man's ability to make progress against the most cunningly planned and powerfully organized opposition.

Without weakening the above statement and taking nothing from the Tulsa Negro's courage, fortitude and resourcefulness, gratitude forces the admission that had it not been for the helping hand of the American Red Cross Society, his morale would have broken and the splendid history he has made since June 1st, 1921, when the savings of a lifetime were reduced to ashes, would have been impossible. That the Red Cross has wrought so nobly in our behalf, is due largely to the spirit of the man in charge, Mr. Maurice Willows.

He is an apostle of the square deal for everyman, regardless of race or color. Behind closed doors in council with bodies of influential white men he fought battles and won victories for us sufficient to merit the everlasting gratitude of our people. The Red Cross as a society, has ministered to our physical needs and Mr. Willows as a man, has stood up for our civic rights at home and a fair presentation of our case abroad. When importuned by interested parties to refer to the eventualities of May 31st and June 1st, in his official report, as a "Negro uprising", he stubbornly refused and instead, called it "the Tulsa disaster" and in addition told the truth as, upon investigation, he found it.

Relief Director, Maurice Willows

While assembled to witness the method by which the Red Cross has elected to give Christmas Cheer to the Negro Children of Tulsa and upon the eve of Mr. Willows' departure from our midst, the undersigned found it fitting to offer these few words of appreciation, on behalf of the entire Negro population of Tulsa, for the unselfish service he has rendered us, with the added assurance that the prayers of a people whom hardship and oppression have thought how to pray will follow him and his associates wherever, in response to the call of suffering humanity and in the line of duty, they may go.

EAST END RELIEF COMMITTEE

Also from the East End Relief Committee

CHRISTMAS TREE

The body of the foregoing report was written prior to the one big event in the lives of the negro children of the devasted district. For the first time in their lives, these hundreds of little folks were without their former comfortable homes. The resources of their parents had been reduced to a point where Christmas could not mean much to them. The workers of the Red Cross staged for them probably the largest Christmas affair ever staged in Tulsa. A beautiful big tree was placed in front of the Red Cross Relief Headquarters. Mr. Chas. Page of Sand Springs kindly furnished the lighting and decorations. The tree was topped with a large cross.

Imagine, if you can, this huge tree brightly lighted standing on Hartford Street in the middle of a district which had once been comfortable homes, but now filled up with little one and two-room wooden shacks with here and there and everywhere large piles of brick and stone, twisted metal and debris, reminding one of the horrible fact of last June. War of the worst sort there had been. The "Maurice Willows hospital" (named such by unanimous vote of the colored people of the district as a measure of their appreciation for what the Red Cross Director has meant to them) stood within a few yards of where the tree was placed. Imagine, if you can, the joy brought to the twenty-seven patients when after dusk on Christmas Eve a Chorus of twenty-two hundred voices sang their Christmas carols and typical negro melodies. Never has the writer witnessed more spontaneous outburst of Christmas fervor than on this occasion. Whole families were there--men, women and children. "Swing Low, Sweet Chariot", "Down By The Ribber Side", "Standing In The Need Of Prayer", coming from the throats of these people, reverberated throughout the night air and attracted most of the crowd gathered in the business section over on Greenwood Street. It seems as tho the whole negro population could not resist the chance to sing.

A liberal supply of candies, nuts and oranges had been tied up into half-pound packages. Twenty-seven hundred of these were distributed in orderly fashion. Individual packages had been prepared suitable to the needs of women and children. These packages had in them everything in the way of useful articles from a spool of thread to a heating stove. Bedsprings, pillows, children's underwear, quilts, cotton bats and every other sort of useful articles were brought by Santa Claus to families which needed these practical things most.

The crowning sentiment of the celebration was in a speech made by one of their leaders who said, "Let us always remember the old negro tradition, there is no room in our hearts for hatred". This occasion furnished what was termed as the "greatest night in the history of Tulsa negroes", and was a fitting culmination of the major relief program of the Red Cross.

1921 Tulsa Race Riot *"Angels of Mercy"*

99

1921 Tulsa Race Riot *"Angels of Mercy"*

1921 Tulsa Race Riot *"Angels of Mercy"*

Believed from the Tulsa World, date not shown..

WILLOWS ENDS HIS RED CROSS WORK

Negroes Give Him Good-bye Meeting in African M. E. Church

Terminating seven months service with the Red Cross doing reconstruction and relief work in the devastated area following the Tulsa race riot, Maurice Willows, director of Red Cross relief left last night for Chicago and New York for a brief trip pending the assuming of his new work in the south. Mrs. Willows and the three children will remain here at least until after school is closed, and will possibly make Tulsa their permanent home.

Willows severs his connection with the Red Cross with the finishing up of the Tulsa job. He will be identified with the Community Service, Incorporated of New York City and goes direct to headquarters with the exception of a brief stop in Chicago from Tulsa. His work will take him south for the late winter and spring months and probably well into the summer.

"I have enjoyed my work in Tulsa," said Willows Monday shortly before his departure, "in all its phases, more than any other work that I have ever done. The Red Cross has for the first time in its history dealt with the race question here in Tulsa and we feel has accomplished its task to the satisfaction of both the white and the colored people."

Willows came to Tulsa Friday, June 4 from divisional headquarters at St. Louis, and took active charge of the relief work and later reconstruction work, as Red Cross director. He leaves with the trustees of this work a complete record of the history of the riot, from the beginning up to December 31, told in his own summarized report, by photographs and newspaper clippings. Four volumes of this report have been prepared; Willows keeps one that will eventually go to the Tulsa trustees; one goes to divisional headquarters at St. Louis; one to national headquarters at Washington and one to the Tulsa chapter of the Red Cross.

Sunday afternoon a great crowd of negroes gathered in the African M. E. church to bid Willows good-bye. Earnest and in many cases tearful assurances of gratitude and affection for him were given by the speakers. Willows leaves a staff of three workers at relief headquarters to carry the work through the winter months.

1921 Tulsa Race Riot *"Angels of Mercy"*

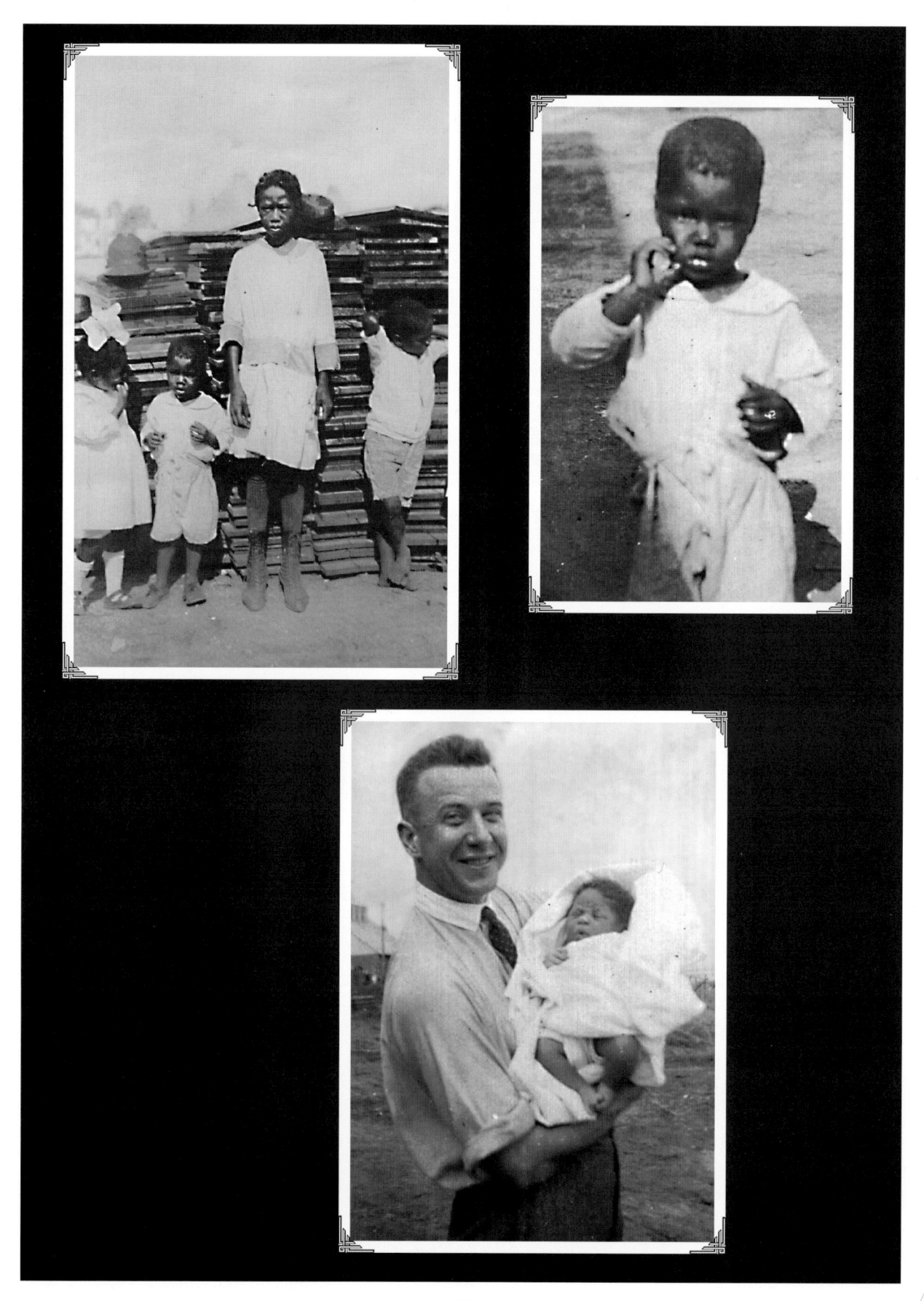

102

1921 Tulsa Race Riot *"Angels of Mercy"*

The following two documents indicate Red Cross policy regarding strikes and riots, prior to the Tulsa Race Riot

Mt. Zion Baptist Church

1921 Tulsa Race Riot "Angels of Mercy"

Letter dated June 1, 1921 from James L. Fieser, Manager of the Southwestern Division of the American Red Cross, to Mr. A. L. Farmer, Chairman of the Tulsa County Chapter, reminding him of the then current Red Cross Policy regarding race riots and strikes.

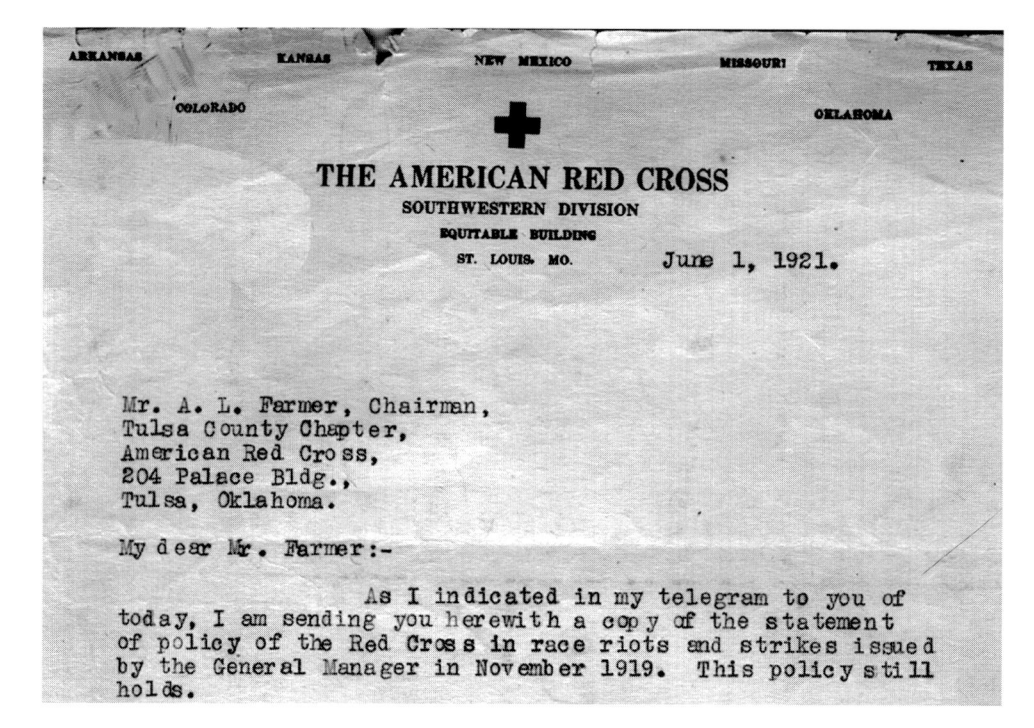

Mr. A.L. Farmer,
Chairman,
Tulsa County
Chapter,
American Red
Cross,
204 Palace Bldg.,
Tulsa, Oklahoma

My dear Mr. Farmer: --

    As I indicated in my telegram of today, I am sending you herewith a copy of the statement of policy of the Red Cross in race riots and strikes issued by the General Manager in November 1919. This policy still holds.

    Unquestionably there is a big opportunity for misunderstanding any action taken by the Red Cross in connection with race riots. One or another party to the situation usually misunderstands and it accordingly becomes necessary for the Red Cross to act with unusual caution. As outlined in the attached statement from the General Manager, Red Cross can best serve through meeting the needs in the form of First Aid, Medical Assistance, Nursing Service, etc.,to those injured in disturbances, regardless of the faction to which they may belong.

    Service should only be rendered to National Guardsmen on the specific request of the State Authorities in charge.

    May I ask that you keep me fully advised on any action taken by your Chapter and particularly in the event that any border line question arises which, in your judgment, does not seem to be covered by the enclosed statement of policy.

    Very sincerely yours,

    James L. Fieser
    Manager, Southwestern Division

This letter makes it clear that the Tulsa Riot was the first such Red Cross experience with a man-made disaster. The riot was in it's second day when this letter was written. The Policy referred to in the letter appears on the next page and again in Mr. Willows' Official Report, which is included in it's entirety in a later section.

1921 Tulsa Race Riot "Angels of Mercy"

(Copy)

POSTAL TELEGRAM

Washington, D. C., Nov. 4. 1919.

Alfred Fairbank,
American Red Cross, Frisco Bldg.,
St. Louis, Mo.

The various situations that have arisen in United States at this time of unrest and readjustment make it desirable we lay before our Division Managers for their personal guidance the attitude which should govern Red Cross in event of race riots and conditions arising out of lockouts and strikes.
Red Cross stands in a peculiar position because of its close relationship to Federal government and at same time because of its support by the American people as a whole, a position which involves both special responsibilities and special obligations. Red Cross must therefore very keenly have in mind its obligations to maintain a position of impartiality. Red Cross must also always be open to appeal to meet needs in form of First Aid, medical assistance, nursing service, etc. to those injured in disturbances regardless of faction to which they may belong. This is the prime service of Red Cross. There are also possible situations where widespread distress may develop as result of conflict between elements in communities, affecting in some cases other than those a party to the disturbance. This type of question may demand action on the part of Red Cross, but decision cannot be made in advance as the possibilities are too various and intricate. Situations do not develop so rapidly but that there remains time for discussion in each case as to the obligation if any on part of Red Cross. There remains a type of service less important but one which Red Cross must consider; this is an obligation to be prepared at all times to furnish certain types of service to Federal troops and to a lesser degree to those who perform types of service similar to those of our army.

1921 Tulsa Race Riot *"Angels of Mercy"*

(Postal Telegram. Washington, D. C.,. Nov. 4, 1919.)

Alfred Fairbank. -- 2.

This is a type of service which should not be sought by Red Cross on its own initiative but a service which should be given in response to request of those in authority. If those in command United States troops make request upon Red Cross for canteen or other reasonable service for the troops themselves, Red Cross should endeavor to meet those demands, confining their efforts strictly to comfort for the soldiers. In the case of state troops our relations are by no means so well worked out and established by war time experience and charter obligation; however, upon request of governor of any state, Red Cross should consider favorably a call for service similar to that which it would be our obligation to render Federal troops limiting service in same way. Beyond this point Red Cross should consider very carefully before undertaking any form of comfort and aid to those engaged in general police duty, being very sure that any request upon them for service is made on behalf of governmental authority representative of the general public and that the type of service requested is limited strictly to giving personal comfort to servants of the public and that such service be closely confined to it proper purposes and not be enlarged in such extent as for practical purposes to amount to furnishing police service of any kind whatsoever. Under no circumstances should this service be rendered to any group in control of either party to a controversy no matter what the temptation, on contrary it should be our aim to make clear and definite the understanding that irrespective of the merits of any controversy Red Cross will avoid favoring either side to that controversy by acts either of commission or omission. It is evident any question of relief which grows out of conflict between different elements in the population a position of much

(Postal Telegram. Washington, D. C., Non. 4, 1919,)

Alfred Fairbank. -- 3.

delicacy to Red Cross with its desire to represent an entire public calls for closest consultation between Chapters and Divisions and Divisions and National Headquarters as to application particularly as such types of controversy affect more than local situations and often involve questions national in scope.

       F. C. Munroe.

1921 Tulsa Race Riot *"Angels of Mercy"*

Relief Director's View of The "Disaster"

WILLOWS' PERSONAL ACCOUNT

Mr. Willows was born in Clinton, Canada, April 16, 1876. He died in a veterans' hospital in Santa Monica, California in January, 1953.

Shortly before his death Mr. Willows wrote a lengthy, well researched history of the Willows family for his children. Along with a listing of his ancestors, he outlined his work history, including his Red Cross work in Tulsa. His personal account, published here for the first time, indicates how he felt obliged to deviate from official Red Cross policy.

Mr. Willows' "official" Red Cross Report is in a later section.

Maurice Willows
1876-1953

1921 Tulsa Race Riot *"Angels of Mercy"*

In 1951, not long before he died, Maurice Willows did considerable research on the Willows family history. The lengthy document, which he wrote for family consumption, included his own work history, and his Red Cross experience with the Tulsa Riot.
To his family, he revealed more of his personal feelings about what happened in that riot than he had included in his official Red Cross Report.
Here is what he said:

I had sensed that back in the National office, certain changes on top levels of future Red Cross policy were in the making. Looking ahead, I saw a return to the peace time program of the organization which would mean the elimination of professional social workers as the controlling influence of future programs. It seems that, without any knowledge of it, the personnel manager of the National Recreation Association was on my trail! It was known as Community Service at the time. By appointment with him in Kansas City, he offered me the same salary as I was getting from the A.R.C. It was a strangely supported organization, with immense possibilities for advancement, and I accepted.

This is in May 1921. I was to begin with them on June 1st. Again, this was not to be. I had closed up with the Red Cross on May 31st. Good Byes were said and left the ARC office, ready for the new job.

Providence, or something else, intervened. On the night of that day Tulsa, Okla. had a night long race riot on. The Tulsa chapter of the Red Cross had been busy imploring Washington to send someone to them. The Washington headquarters called St. Louis. The St. Louis people contacted the Recreation Association, which called off my first trip for them. The Red Cross was in the saddle again. Instead of taking a day train for New York on the 1st of June, I was shunted on a night one TULSA bound, still a Red Cross employee! This is where Tulsa came in!

On the morning of June 2nd, 1921, I dropped off the Frisco at 7.30 A.M. The city was stunned by what had happened. Crowds of both whites and negroes were milling about. In front of the Y.M.C.A. building was a crowd of negroes being fed, handout fashion. Their homes had been burned out, families had been scattered and no one seemed to have authority in control. At ten thirty A.M. a meeting was held in the city hall, where a citizens committee was formed.

For good reasons, the committee was composed of leading white citizens, minus any city officials. On account of local (and embarrassing) complications, the Red Cross man was asked to take charge of the relief situation. Before committing myself, or the Red Cross, it seemed clear that the trouble did not have any providential causes, and, as the Red Cross had never taken a hand in man made disasters, I called Washington with the report that: there was an unknown number of homeless refugees, all negroes; there was no adequate relief organization in town; on account of the divisions between the whites and negroes, a political situation complicated everything, etc, etc, WHAT should I do?

Mr. Persons (still at the head) said, "We will take your advice- GO Ahead- and report further, we will back you". Thus, all in a brief few hours, the work began. At a noon meeting of the Citizens Committee I gave the following report: That the Red Cross would help out, but the understanding should be clear and positive. First: That the relief " administration" would be financed by the National Red Cross. (This in order to ward off interference by local people who might have political or racial feelings involved). Second: That the city and county of Tulsa would finance ALL relief needs. Third: That the incumbent city officials (the Mayor and Police

1921 Tulsa Race Riot *"Angels of Mercy"*

Chief included) should abdicate for a period of sixty days, and that the Citizens Committee should be in the city hall saddle for the time being.

The Chairman of the committee was a superior court judge, and the propositions stated were agreed to. The work of relief had already begun. From that time on we had little trouble. The National office, on receiving a satisfactory report, asked me what I wanted from them. I replied, " $25,000 for administration and personnel purposes only. "O.K." came the answer. In a day or two I had a relief staff of several local social workers at work, and others from a distance on the way. We appointed the local oil industry purchasing agent to handle all purchasing matters; a local accountant to look after bookkeeping matters and other local persons for minor staff places. In order to steer clear of any possible dictatorship implications, the following safeguards were set up: A leading physician (Dr. Brown) was made head of the medical relief. The Visiting Nurses Ass'n headed up the nursing service (under Dr. Brown). The local acting chairman of of the local Red Cross chapter (Clark Field) was my chief advisor on current matters of policy. With this set up, we proceeded.

To those of you who do not know, or remember Tulsa at the time, the negro district bordered on the east and north of the Santa Fe R.R. tracks and immediately north of the Frisco R.R. tracks.

This whole district was a shamble. Little was left but unburned chimneys. A few businesses and houses remained as did the Washington (negro) school. An unknown number of fatalities had occurred, while nearly two thousand men, women and children had been driven out of town

or had to be cared for by the relief organization. Temporarily, the city auditorium, the baseball park, sheds, church basements , etc., were used for housing. The remaining school building was used as a hospital. Local hospitals helped as far as their accommodations would permit. Lumber for rebuilding purposes was a first essential. Local lumber concerns had limited stocks of the kind of material that we wanted. Our purchasing agent went to nearby mills and bought two carloads of lumber. Local negro carpenters were provided the lumber, they did the work of building homes. There being no negro hospital, one had to be built. The schools had to be reopened soon and the school house vacated for its own purpose.

A workshop was set up in tents for the women folks, equipped with sewing machines, etc. We went to St. Louis and bought a car load of household necessities, also dry goods which were provided the women. Briefly, we furnished all necessary for the negroes to rehabilitate themselves, requiring themselves to work it all out! In a very short time a temporary hospital was finished. It cost around $6,000 (city money). It is the first negro hospital in OKLA. The negroes named it

1921 Tulsa Race Riot *"Angels of Mercy"*

Local negro carpenters built temporary homes.

the "Maurice Willows Hospital". The name was still used long after I left, and until a fine brick structure replaced it several years after.

Maurice Willows Hospital, "The first non - private negro hospital in Tulsa."

It was a modest building, but well equipped even had a fine operating room. Our nurses were whites, and the negro patients were given as good treatment as any patients in any man's hospital. Dr. Brown was our Chief Doctor and medical advisor, a Dr. Smith, Tulsa's leading surgeon was on the staff too.

The hospital was on the same ground as our office and workshop, which meant that I was having a wonderful experience along the administration line.

Following the sixty days, when the city officials were laying low, we had some legal squabbles. We were getting those refugees back into their homes. The city council passed an ordinance which would prevent the building of anything but fireproof buildings.

The negroes could not afford the more expensive houses and we would not agree to the restrictions levied. Our attorneys, headed by a wonderful Judge (Eakes) fought the council and WON hands down!

1921 Tulsa Race Riot "Angels of Mercy"

So you will know something of the background of the trouble and the causes. The negro people had been segregated in their district for many years. Many of them owned their property. They had their own business section, school and churches. The section was valuable, and as the Tulsa population grew, it became more so.

Red Cross operating room.

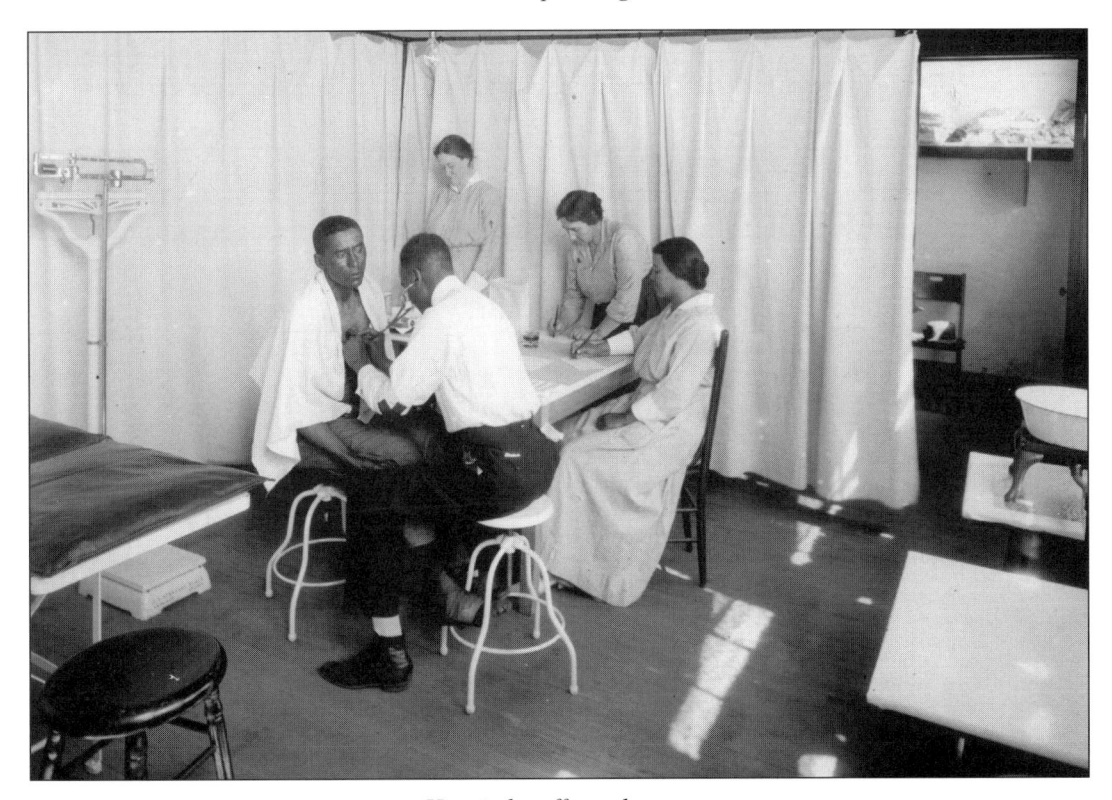

Hospital staff members.

1921 Tulsa Race Riot "Angels of Mercy"

A few conscienceless real estate men tried to get a deal with another few negroes whereby the district could be taken over in a few years by business interests. The plan was to remove the district farther out into the suburbs. The negro people of influence would not countenance the underground attempts made to oust them, which would mean a sacrifice of their strategic location, built up by hard work, and much less the acceptance of mere pittances offered for their home properties. The city government was not what one might call a "virtuous" one.

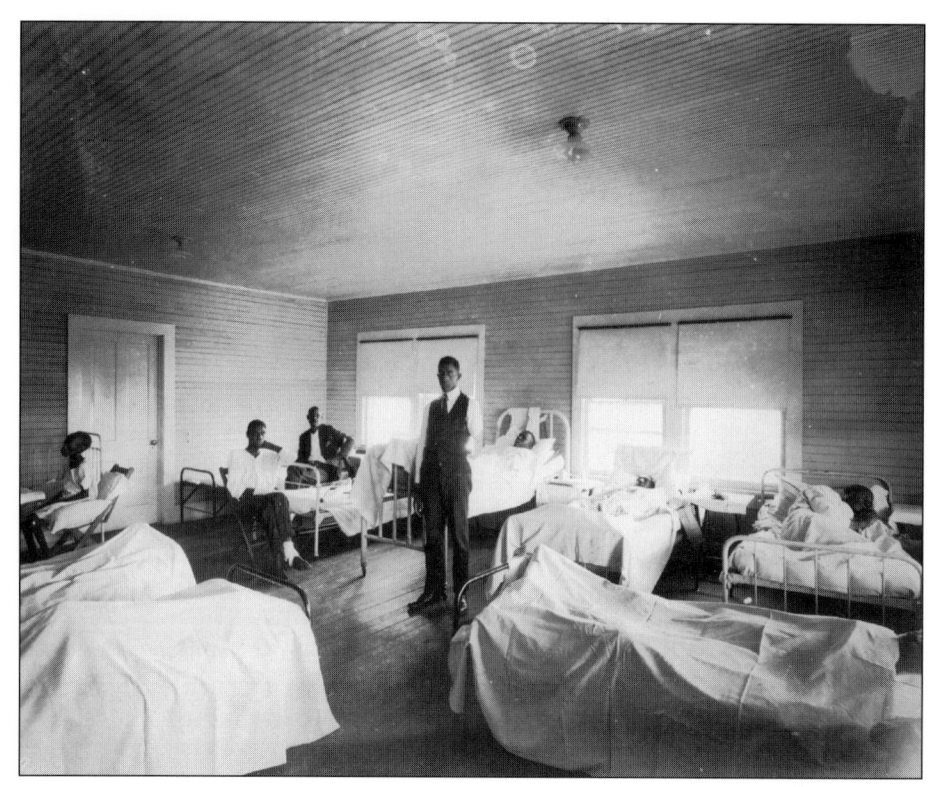

Hospital Ward

Maurice Willows Hospital

Tulsa, at the time had much unemployment, many negro families were having a hard time of it, as everyone was during depression periods. It was figured (by the underground hoodlums) that this was a good time to STRIKE the blow that would drive the negroes to locate in another district. They recruited (the hoodlum gang) a lot of ne'er-do-wells into the ugly conspiracy to burn out the district.

1921 Tulsa Race Riot *"Angels of Mercy"*

Many conflicting stories were told as to HOW the fires were started on the night of May 31st, but during the night the whole negro district had been pillaged first and burned up afterwards.

The negroes fled, men and women carrying their children with them, with no time to take any of their belongings with them. This was NOT a RIOT, as some of the out of town papers called it in their screaming headlines of the next day. It was a well planned, diabolical ouster of the innocent negroes from their stamping grounds. The planners were key persons in both races, in and with the knowledge of the police, and even reaching into officialdom in the city hall.

Typical wooden shack.

If you can get or see copies of the Tulsa papers for the month of June 1921, you will see pictures of armed men on the downtown street corners, chasing every negro in sight. OH! YES! They had their ALIBI ! A negro boy was supposed to have attempted an assault on a white woman in a downtown elevator, and the enraged whites had an excuse for their manufactured rage. The negro was jailed for weeks but was released after no truthful evidence was produced against him.

Too bad that there was no Kefauver investigating committee on the job! It was not in our province to unwrap causes. It was ours to care for the wounded, hospitalize the mothers and children, get them into homes again!

The above poorly told story would not be complete without comment:

1. It took seven months of hard work on the part of the Red Cross and many volunteers to get to a place where the negroes could be depended upon to carry on themselves.

2. The City and County had spent nearly $200,000 (two hundred thousand), of tax money for relief and rehabilitation.

3. The Red Cross headquarters staff carried on within the amount originally appropriated, ($25,000), at the end of which time a report was made in triplicate, one volume going to Washington, another to the local Red Cross chapter and the third being kept by myself. The report contained all vital information on the affair from the beginning to the end of operations. The volume also included newspaper clippings of the affair.

1921 Tulsa Race Riot *"Angels of Mercy"*

Red Cross Relief supply room at Washington school.

4. During the operations we had the solid good will and cooperation of all the citizenry, both white and colored folks. Even the few politicians who were involved, had become quiet and uncritical.

5. At the time of our shutting up shop, a joint mass meeting of both whites and negroes was held, at which time the A.R.C. and its relief staff were showered with thanks.

Supply room next to new Maurice Willows hospital.

6. This was the only deviation of Red Cross policy on record. When my first report was made to the Citizens Committee, the causes were not entirely clear, but clear enough to warrant placing the financial responsibility for relief on the City and County of Tulsa. Not on the ARC or relief fund campaign. The public was approving, as it was common knowledge that the City government was shot through with political corruption and inter-racial connivances.

7. The best elements, among both the whites and negroes, were satisfied with the ARC coming because there was no local group who could cope with the delicate situation. After it was all over and our departure, NOT ONE VOICE was raised because of the TAX money being spent as it was.

8. In the meantime, public opinion had been crystallizing in favor of civic pride and decency. There was an accounting time coming! At the next municipal election, the ballots ousted the whole city hall outfit. Other retributions followed. Tate Brady, a political henchman who was a leader among the trouble makers, committed suicide. Buck Lewis (a real estate man with greedy intentions) met a violent death. Another had to leave Tulsa, and others had a family breakup.

Red Cross Purchasing Department.

AFTERMATH: A few years afterwards, I visited the area and found civic improvements on all sides: paved streets, gas and water facilities installed, improved schools, a new hospital, etc.
Good!

1921 Tulsa Race Riot   *"Angels of Mercy"*

Disaster Relief Report

1921 Tulsa Race Riot "Angels of Mercy"

DISASTER RELIEF REPORT

The following section is a copy of Mr. Willows' official report on Red Cross relief of what they called, "The Tulsa Disaster." Some of it was included in previous sections with related visuals.

I am grateful to Mr. Probes and the Tulsa Chapter of the American Red Cross for their cooperation and encouragement. I deeply regret Mr. Probes died before this book was completed. He was justly proud of Red Cross Relief following the Tulsa Race Riot, and would be pleased the "Angels of Mercy" story is being told.

Mr. Willow's "personal" account of his seven month duty in Tulsa appeared in the previous section.

INDEX

ORGANIZATION	PERSONNEL
ORGANIZATION	RELIEF ORDERS
REPORT	MAURICE WILLOWS
SUPPLEMENT TO GENERAL REPORT	MAURICE WILLOWS
MISCELLANEOUS DOCUMENTS	
CLIPPINGS	
PHOTOGRAPHS AND SNAPSHOTS	

ORGANIZATION

Proclamation of Mayor of Tulsa

Instructions from Chairman of Red Cross, Southwestern Division

National Guard Field Orders

Orders to Physicians Committee

Orders to Boy Scouts

Employment Organization

Identification Tags, Meal Tickets, etc.

Minutes of Meeting of Medical Committee

REPORT

TULSA RACE RIOT

DISASTER RELIEF

AMERICAN RED CROSS

COMPILED BY
LOULA V. WATKINS.

This compilation contains copies and duplicates of the original texts now in the possession of Mr. Maurice Willows, Director of Relief, Disaster Relief Headquarters, American Red Cross, Tulsa, Oklahoma.

Besides the compilation made for Mr. Willows by Mrs. Loula V. Watkins, there are three others - one for Tulsa, one for Washington, and one for St. Louis Red Cross files.

The typing was done by Miss Cleda Timberlake of Denver, Colorado. Most of the snapshots were contributed by Mr. Clarence H. Dawson, of Chicago.

The Compiler

1921 Tulsa Race Riot *"Angels of Mercy"*

FAMILY RELIEF PERSONNEL

Clarence H. Dawson, Director - - Chicago, Ill.

CASE WORKERS

Abbot, Mrs. Gretchen	- - -	Tulsa, Okla.
Fish, Mrs. Ruth G.	- - -	Alamosa, Colo.
Mac Cartney, Mrs. C. B.	- - -	Oklahoma City, Okla.
Prout, Miss Jeanne	- - -	Memphis, Tenn.
Scott, Miss Mary Porter	- - -	St. Louis, Mo.
Watkins, Mrs. L. V.	- - -	Kirkwood, Mo.
Westendorf, Miss Katharine	- - -	Denver, Colo.

The following workers served only during the emergency period immediately following the riot.

Adams, Mr. C. D.	- - -	Tulsa, Okla.
Davis, Miss Dorothy	- - -	Houston, Texas
Golay, Mrs. T. L.	- - -	Tulsa, Okla.
Lefko, Mr. Louis	- - -	Tulsa, Okla.
Palmer, Miss Ada	- - -	Chicago, Ill.
Reed, Mrs. J. M.	- - -	Tulsa, Okla.
Williams, Miss Margaret	- - -	St. Louis, Mo.

STENOGRAPHERS

Timberlake, Miss Cleda	- - -	Denver, Colo.
Leslie, Miss Mildred	- - -	Tulsa, Okla.
Beggs, Miss	- - -	Tulsa, Okla.
O'Brien, Miss	- - -	Tulsa, Okla.
Miss Marguerite Watkins	- - -	Tulsa, Okla.

OFFICE CHIEF EXECUTIVE

T. D. EVANS, MAYOR

TULSA, OKLAHOMA

To The Red Cross Society:

Please establish headquarters for all relief work and bring all organizations who can assist you to your aid. The responsibility is placed in your hands entirely.

                (signed) T. D. Evans,
                                Mayor

6/2/21

1921 Tulsa Race Riot *"Angels of Mercy"*

THE AMERICAN RED CROSS
SOUTHWESTERN DIVISION
ST. LOUIS, MO

June 1, 1921

Mr. A. L. Farmer, Chairman,
Tulsa County Chapter
American Red Cross
204 Palace Bldg.
Tulsa, Oklahoma

My Dear Mr. Farmer:-

     As I indicated in my telegram to you of today, I am sending you herewith a copy of the statement of policy of the Red Cross in race riots and strikes issued by the General Manager in November 1919. This policy still holds.

     Unquestionably there is big opportunity for misunderstanding any action taken by the Red Cross in connection with race riots. One or another party to the situation usually misunderstands and it accordingly becomes necessary for the Red Cross to act with unusual caution. As outlined in the attached statement from the General Manager, Red Cross can best serve through meeting the needs in the form of First Aid, Medical Assistance, Nursing Service, etc., to those injured in disturbances, regardless of the faction to which they may belong.

     Service should only be rendered to National Guardsmen on the specific request of the State Authorities in charge.

     May I ask that you keep me fully advised of any action taken by your Chapter and particularly in the event that any border line question arises which, in your judgement, does not seem to be covered by the enclosed statement of policy.

     Very sincerely yours,

     James L. Fieser,
     Manager, Southwestern Division.

JLF*S

1921 Tulsa Race Riot *"Angels of Mercy"*

(COPY)

<u>(POSTAL TELEGRAM)</u>　　　　　　　　　　　　Washington, D.C. Nov. 4, 1919

Alfred Fairbank,
American Red Cross, Frisco Bldg.
St. Louis, Mo.

The various situations that have arisen in United States at this time of unrest and readjustment make it desirable we lay before our Division Managers for their personal guidance the attitude which should govern Red Cross in event of race riots and conditions arising out of lockouts and strikes. Red Cross stands in a peculiar position because of it close relationship to Federal Government and at same time because of its support by the American people as a whole, a position which involves both special responsibilities and special obligations. Red Cross must therefore very keenly have in mind its obligations to maintain a position of impartiality. Red Cross must also always be open to appeal to meet needs in form of First Aid, medical assistance, nursing services, etc. to those injured in disturbances regardless of faction to which they may belong. This is the prime service of Red Cross. There are also possible situations where widespread distress may develop as result of conflict between elements in communities, affecting in some cases other than those a party to the disturbance. This type or question may demand action on the part of Red Cross, but decision cannot be made in advance as the possibilities are too various and intricate. Situations do not develop so rapidly but that there remains time for discussion in each case as to the obligation if any on part of Red Cross. There remains a type of service less important but one which Red Cross must consider; this is an obligation to be prepared at all times to furnish certain types of service similar to those of our army. This is a type of service which should not be sought by Red Cross on its own

(Postal Telegram. Washington, D. C., Nov. 4, 1919.)

Alfred Fairbank - 2.

initiative but a service which should be given in response to request of those in authority. If those in command United States troops make request upon Red Cross for canteen or other reasonable service for the troops themselves, Red Cross should endeavor to meet these demands, confining their efforts strictly to comfort for the soldiers. In the case of state troops our relations are by no means so well worked out and established by war time experience and charter obligation; however, upon request of governor of any state, Red Cross should consider favorably a call for service similar to that which it would be our obligation to render Federal troops limiting service in same way. Beyond this point Red Cross should consider very carefully before undertaking any form of comfort and aid to those engaged in general police duty, being very sure that any request upon them for service is made on behalf of governmental authority representative of the general public and that the type of service requested is limited strictly to giving personal comfort to servants of the public and that such service be closely confined to its proper purposes and not be enlarged in such extent as for practical purposes to amount to furnishing police service of any kind whatsoever. Under no circumstances should this service be rendered to any group in control of either party to a controversy no matter what the temptation, on contrary it should be our aim to make clear and definite the understanding that irrespective of the merits of any controversy Red Cross will avoid favoring either side to that controversy by acts either of commission or omission. It is evident any question of relief which grows out of conflict between different elements in the population a position of much delicacy to Red Cross with its desire to represent an entire public calls for closes consultation

(Postal Telegram, Washington, D. C. Nov. 4, 1919.)

Alfred Fairbank - 3.

between delicacy to Red Cross with its desire to represent an entire public calls for closest consultation between Chapters and Divisions and Divisions and National Headquarters as to application particularly as such types of controversy affect more than local situations and often involve questions national in scope.

                              F. C. Munroe.

1921 Tulsa Race Riot *"Angels of Mercy"*

HEADQUARTERS OKLAHOMA NATIONAL GUARD

TULSA, OKLAHOMA   JUNE 2, 1921.

Field Order No. __4__

All the able bodied negro men remaining in detention camp at Fair Grounds and other places in the City of Tulsa will be required to render such service and perform such labor as is required by the military commission and the Red Cross in making the proper sanitary provisions for the care of the refugees.

Able bodied women, not having the care of children, will also be required to perform such service as may be required in the feeding and care of the refugees.

This order covers any labor necessary in the care of the health or welfare of these people who, by reason of their misfortunes, must be looked after by the different agencies of relief.

By order of Brig. Gen. Chas. F. Barrett -

Chas. F. Barrett
Brig. Gen.

HEADQUARTERS NATIONAL GUARD

CITY HALL, TULSA, OKLAHOMA, JUNE 2, 1921.

Field Order No. 5.   To Commanding Officer, 3 Infantry. You will detail a Non-Commissioned officer and 18 men to set as guard at Fair Grounds Detention Camp, this detail be armed and fully equipped will report to Clark Field at American Red Cross Headquarters. From and after 1 P.M. this date detention camp at McNulty Camp will abolish and camps will be removed to Detention Camp at Fair Grounds.

> By Command of Brig. Gen. Barrett.
>
> Bryon Kirkpatrick
>
> May A. G. Dept. Adj.

June 2, 1921

Chief of Police Gustafson:

Will you kindly furnish us two white police officers, to report at Red Cross Headquarters, Fourth and Cincinnati.

_____

Assist. Director.

1921 Tulsa Race Riot *"Angels of Mercy"*

Tulsa, Okla.
June 5th, 1921

The Physicians Committee of the Board of Public Health recognizes and accepts the selection of Chief of Department as made by the American Red Cross as follows, i.e.

Surgery	Dr. Ralph V. Smith
Obstetrics	Dr. George R. Osborn
Medicine	Dr. Horace T. Price

For immediate service the following Doctors may be called:

Surgery	Dr. H. D. Murdock	0 - 95
	Dr. A. W. Pigford	0 - 187
	Dr. H. S. Browne	C - 1039
	Dr. D. C. Johnson	0 - 5011
	Dr. G. H. Miller	0 - 6669
Medicine	Dr. A. G. Wainwright	C - 497
	Dr. C. S. Summers	0 - 9160
	Dr. W. J. Trainer	0 - 8744
	Dr. J. E. Wallace	0 - 812
	Dr. E. B. Wilson	0 - 8727
Obstetrics	Dr. Geo R. Osborn	0 - 2010

It is the purpose of this committee to work in harmony with the American Red Cross and the other organizations doing relief work.

In recognition of the valuable services performed by Dr. Paul R. Browne, we recommend that in case of need he be consulted by all chiefs of departments and this committee.

The committee requests that the various types of work outlined further on, at the places named by performed by the designated physicians.

Sanitation - Dr. C. L. Reeder, Dr. L. C. Presson and assistants shall be responsible for sanitation through the city and county.

Fair Grounds Camp - Dr. C. D. Johnson, A. C. Wainwright and assistants shall have charge of all medical and surgical cases at the Fair Grounds Camp, but sending all Major operative cases to the Morningside Hospital and others requiring hospitalization to the Red Cross Hospital.

Obstetrics - Dr. Geo. R. Osborn and Assistants shall take care of all obstetrical cases arising anywhere, which must be sent in time to the Tulsa or Oklahoma Hospitals.

Red Cross Hospital - Dr. R. B. Smith and Assistants shall have charge of all operative cases at the Morningside and Red Cross Hospitals. Dr. C. H. Haralson and assistants shall take care of all eye, ear, nose, and throat cases arising anywhere which may require special attention and those now in or coming to the Morningside or Red Cross Hospitals.

Booker Washington First Aid Station - Dr. Geo. H. Miller, Dr. C. S. Summers and assistants shall be responsible for the first aid and after treatment of all cases applying to this dispensary.

The Committee recommends that no attempt be made to rebuild the devastated area until a sanitary sewerage system has been installed, with connections to each building or that it shall at least be started and no building planned without such connections and accessories, within the corporate limits of the City.

We further recommend that the adjacent territory now situated in the county, be immediately included within the corporate limits in order that the health of the community may be protected by the installation of proper sewerage.

We further recommend that recognizing the extremely insanitary conditions existing within the devastated area, that if legally possible, the same be corrected through condemnatory proceedings and necessary destruction of all shacks that are now a menace to health.

In view of the fact that their building and equipment have been destroyed by fire, we recommend that temporary quarters be provided in the colored district for the use of the Tulsa County Public Health Association, that is work may be resumed at once and we further recommend that permanent quarters be provided as soon as possible. We further recommend that the tuberculosis and general public health work be resumed at once among the white population at the Public Health dispensary, 15 West 11th St.

    By Order of the Committee

        Dr. C. L. Reeder, Chairman

        Dr. R. V. Smith

        Dr. Horace T. Price, Secy.

1921 Tulsa Race Riot *"Angels of Mercy"*

TULSA   COUNCIL

BOY SCOUTS   OF AMERICA

TULSA   OKLAHOMA

REQUEST FOR SCOUT SERVICES

Number of Scouts Needed ----------------------------------

Nature of Service.

Remarks.

TULSA COUNCIL

BOY SCOUTS OF AMERICAN

TULSA OKLAHOMA

Washington School

INFORMATION ABOUT BOY SCOUT SERVICE

1. EACH OFFICE WILL HAVE A DETAIL OF SCOUTS FOR SERVICES IN THE BUILDING CONSISTING OF A DOOR ORDERLY AND ONE OR MORE DESK ORDERLIES.

2. THE DOOR ORDERLY SHALL NOT BE ORDERED FROM HIS POST BY ANY ONE OTHER THAN THE SCOUT DIRECTOR.

3. THE DESK ORDERLIES ARE FOR SERVICE INSIDE THE BUILDING ONLY.

4. SCOUTS ARE ON RESERVE IN THE SCOUT DIRECTORS OFFICE FOR ALL OTHER DUTIES.

5. ALL REQUESTS FOR SCOUTS SHOULD BE MADE IN PERSON OR BY A WRITTEN ORDER STATING THE NUMBER OF SCOUTS DESIRED AND THE NATURE OF SERVICE REQUESTED.

6. NO SCOUT SHALL LEAVE THE BUILDING WITHOUT A WRITTEN ORDER FROM THE SCOUT DIRECTOR.

(signed)   F. D. Craft.

EMPLOYMENT ORGANIZATION

Duties of Agencies.

Red Cross Representative

    Refers calls of all kinds to proper agency.
    Makes Adjustments.
    Forms contact with Red Cross Committee
    Special advertising.

Federal State Employment Bureau

    Direct all employment work.
    Fill all calls for permanent male colored.
    Labor and day work for colored women.

Colored Y. M. C. A.

    Fill all calls for day work for colored men.

Colored Y. W. C. A.

    Fill all calls for permanent work for colored women.

General Activities

    Committee meeting Tuesday, 2:00 p.m. Washington School.

    Employment city survey for positions.

    Placards all over colored district, calling attention to agencies operating.

    Advertising by newspaper stories.

EMPLOYMENT ORGANIZATION

Red Cross Representative:
    N. A. Thompson, Cedar 2300, Washington School House

Employment Committee:
    Chairman W. R. Ellis, Osage 3540, 14 1/2 E. First St.
        Representing Federal State Employment Service.

    G. A. Gregg, Cedar 615. Easton and Axter
        Representing Colored Y.M.C.A.

    Edna Pyle, Archer and Cincinnati,
        Representing Y.W.C.A.

    Miss Hloise Williams, Osage 8639, 4th & Cincinnati.
        Representing Y.W.C.A.

    Mrs. Victor A. Hunt, Osage 8823, 5th & Cheyenne.
        Representing Y.W.C.A.

    Barney Meyers, Osage 9393, 120 W. Third St.
        Representing Open Shop Ass'n.

    G. F. James,
        Representing Central Labor Unions.

    T. C. Hopkins, Osage 9720, 406 So. Cincinnati.
        Representing American Legion.

1921 Tulsa Race Riot *"Angels of Mercy"*

June 6, 1921

Report from Medical Committee.

Report on Financial matters. Arranged that Fields, Terrell and Avery should arrange handling of funds and distribution of funds.

Matter of feeding taken up. Decided all dependents should go to fair grounds and all mass feeding done there. Reported that arrangements had been made at Booker Washington school to feed all workmen over there for 15 cents per meal and deduct it from wages.

Graham suggested getting all superfluous people out of white residence section, and issuing permanent passes to and from the fair grounds to responsible working people and daily passes to others. Question of jitney service to and from fair grounds for working people, and question of supplies for semi-permanent camp taken up.

Kates moved that Graham and Maj. Fuller be instructed to confer with Executive Committee, with full power on the part of Graham and Fuller to act with the Executive Committee to get all excess people out of servants' questers and move them to the fair grounds - to act with Central Committee and Mr. Terrell.

Mr. Fields asked Kates to include motion to feed refugees and issue passes.

Kates moved to give Graham and Fuller complete authority to work out any scheme that is advisable to them and the Executive Committee and police identifying refugees by card, keeping off streets, moving, etc.

Willows stated that was not a matter which should be settled by Red Cross themselves, and whatever action is taken should be taken conjointly, in order that a united front might be presented to the people.

Kates stated that motion included recommendation for jitney service and everything else.

Willows stated that this would be placed in the hands of these men, to report back tonight.

Motion seconded, and upon vote unanimously adopted.

Question of setting up stands and stores taken up. Chief Police stated Hopkins was handling that.

Mr. Fields: At first we had a clear understanding that the regular funds of the Tulsa Chapter were not to be put with this relief fund, as St. Louis informed us that their manner of handling relief funds is to handle it as separate from Chapter funds until all other resources are

-2-

exhausted and then, if necessary, use our Chapter funds and then go back on St. Louis.

Mr. Willows: Our understanding with the Committee was, get your bills together and when you need money to pay them, bring them to us.

Question of employment taken. Decided to consolidate with all other employment agencies and it was suggested that Chairman of State Federal Employment Agency be Chairman of such Committee. Mr. Ireland to handle this matter as he sees fit.

Question of payroll taken up. Any one who is to be paid out of Red Cross Funds to report to Murray or Willows.

Kates brought up question of fire protection at fair grounds and Police Chief said they were attending to it.

Fields stated he would like Central Committee put on record as requesting them to feed workmen.

Murray reported that Borden is going to put on an inventory man and going to take an inventory of all Red Cross stuff.

Willows asked police to take action on matter of supplying transportation for negroes backwards and forwards over and around town, and to take action to stop this transportation by whites.

1921 Tulsa Race Riot *"Angels of Mercy"*

STATEMENT OF THE PASTORS OF THE CITY OF TULSA

The fair name of the city of Tulsa has been tarnished and blackened by a crime that ranks with the dastardly deeds of the Germans during the Great War, provoked by the bad element of the negroes, arming themselves and marching through the streets of the city. Block hand of the mob. Many of our people are dead, while thousands of innocent, peaceable, and law-abiding citizens have not only been rendered homeless, but they have been robbed and despoiled of all their earthly possessions. The pastors of Tulsa blush for shame at this outrage which renders our city odious and condemned before the world.

We believe that the only bulwark of American safety for our liberties, our homes, the peaceful pursuits of happiness, of law, order, and common decency, is found in the teaching and living of the high ideals of Jesus Christ, - that without Christ modern civilization cannot bear the weight that is being placed upon it, and the crash is inevitable.

We, the Pastors of this city, hold that there cannot be peace, security, happiness, moral conscience, to say nothing of religious development, so long as the following obtain:

1. The Bible, God, Jesus Christ, and the Christian Religion outlawed in the Public Schools. It is only where Christianity has influence and power that the Jew and the Infidel are protected. We insist that they have no right to tear down in America that which not only protects them but protects us. The little sop thrown to the Christian forces at Commencement by Prayer and a Sermon is a little more than an insult to Christianity.

While the Bible has been outlined, the Dance has been put into the public schools over the protest of hundreds of fathers and mothers who have a conscience on the subject. Certainly it is an established fact that the dance weakens moral fiber. We therefore demand consideration.

2. A wide open Sunday. The amusement houses, parks, and anything else that desires is free to run wide open on the Lords day. It was respect for the Lords day and the Lords house the built that sturdy New England civilization which gave the world the Declaration of Independence, the Constitution of the United States, the great educational institution of the Eastern part of the United States, as well as the great statesmen, poets, philosophers, and philanthropists.

3. Motion picture houses constantly showing films that are suggestive in title, Poster Advertisement, and in actual production on the screen where there is drinking, the use of weapons, the portrayal of lust, the portrayal of the eternal triangle, the breaking of homes, the caracture of the Christian ministry, - until the young and ignorant get the idea that such is the common order of society. That in 1919, Tulsa County gave the starting total of 56.8 divorces, an increase of 18.9% over 1917, 2 years, is food for solid thought.

4. Officials who can see a car parked a foot out of line, but who are blind to Choc-joints, boot-legging, and the like, said to flourish in and about Tulsa.

5. Officials who have already winked at two lynchings, and who had every opportunity of knowing that a third war contemplated hours before the trouble actually begun.

6. Criminals who are given their freedom almost immediately after arrest either on worthless bonds, or through some powerful "Friend" at court, or through some other unlawful manner.

7. A certain type of citizenship which openly boasts of violating the Law with respect to the 18th Amendment.

We, the Pastors of the City of Tulsa, urge that a thorough and complete investigation of this outrage be made immediately, and that wherever the guilty ones may be found, and whoever they are, white or black, that a full punishment be meted out. Good citizenship can not condone and tolerate vandalism, looting, and such other lawless acts as both black and white were guilty of May 31st, and June 1st. We believe that the possession of firearms and ammunition, especially rifles, revolvers, and such should be made a felony.

We call upon the officials, both County and Municipal, for a full enforcement of the Law. We call for a readjustment of our Moral and Civic life, placing it on the plain of decency, righteousness and justice.

We appeal to the Christians of Tulsa to be more faithful in exemplifying the true meaning of Christianity in word and deed, to refrain from all questionable practices, and to give themselves over to the practice of Christian virtues and general Christian living.

We appeal to the unaffiliated Church members to take membership at once with their respective Churches, for in so doing they will strengthen the moral fibre of the Community. This is no time to hold aloof.

We also deem it the part of wisdom that there should be a closer cooperation between the religious and business forces of the two races in Tulsa, so that at all times there shall be a better mutual understanding making it possible for both races to work together to achieve the highest ideals. As an example of what we have in mind, we have invited the pastors of the Colored churches to associate themselves with the Ministerial Alliance in this city.

We believe most emphatically that the Church is the only hope for the City of Tulsa, and without her moral influence there can be no security no matter how many or what laws are enacted, or how well policed the city may be. The observance of all law depends upon the moral consciousness and the Church is the only Institution in our society whose sole and only business is the creating of that Moral Consciousness.

The Church stands between Society and destruction. What are you doing for the Church?

TULSA MINISTERIAL ALLIANCE.

REPORT

BY MAURICE WILLOWS, DIRECTOR

TULSA   COUNTY   CHAPTER   AMERICAN   RED   CROSS

DISASTER   RELIEF   COMMITTEE

PREFACE

The story of the tragedy enacted in Tulsa, Oklahoma, on the night of May 31st, 1921, the the morning of June 1st, 1921, has been told and retold, with all sorts of variations, in the press of the country. Whatever people choose to call it, "race riot", "massacre", "negro uprising", or whatnot, the word has not yet been coined which can correctly describe the affair.

This report attempts to picture the situation as representatives of the Red Cross found it, and to record the activities of the organization in bringing order out of chaos and in administering relief to the innocents.

(signed)

Director.

1921 Tulsa Race Riot "Angels of Mercy"

CHAPTER I

Months and maybe years will elapse before the inside truth will come to the surface as to the real causes of civil warfare which turned Tulsa, Oklahoma, into a bedlam on the night of May 31st, 1921.

"Race Riot" it has been called, yet whites were killed and wounded by whites, in the protection of white property against the violence of a white mob. The elements of race rioting were there to be sure, but the proportion of negroes killed and wounded testifies to an unequal battle.

The newspapers agree that the local and immediate cause of the trouble began when a negro boy, on entering an elevator conducted by a white girl, stepped on her foot. A frightened girl, - a more frightened negro - a police officer - and the jail. A newspaper headline - some local irritations, - a band of negroes, a larger band of whites, - plenty of guns, and a riot was on, all Tuesday night and until Wednesday noon it raged.

All that fire, rifles, revolvers, machine guns and inhuman bestiality could do with thirty-five city blocks with its ten thousand negro population, was done.

Those interested in details, bearing on locations, methods used, and the organization of the mobs, both block and white, should refer to newspaper accounts of the trial of the Chief of Police, and in addition, newspaper reports directly following the riot, all of which are contained herewith.

DEAD

The number of dead is a matter of conjecture. Some knowing ones estimate the number of killed as high as 300, other estimates being as low as 55. The bodies were hurriedly rushed to burial, and the records of many burials are not to be found.

INJURED

One hundred and eighty four negroes and forty-eight whites were in hospitals for surgical care, within twenty-four hours. Five hundred and thirty-one were given First Aid at the Red Cross Stations during the first three days following the affair.

An adequate picture of conditions relating to the injured cannot be written. Eye witnesses will long remember the speeding ambulances, the crowed hospitals, drugstores, churches and First Aid Stations. While the records show 763 wounded, this does not include wounded people afterwards found on practically all roads leading out of Tulsa. Wounded people turned up at Muskogee, Sapulpa, and other adjoining towns, and as far north as Kansas City. Neither do records tell of the after-the-riot developments. The Red Cross records show eight definite causes of premature childbirth which resulted in the death of the babies.

Subsequent developments also show that of the maternity cases known to the Red Cross Doctors, practically all have presented complications due to the riot.

Too much credit cannot be given to the white citizens of Tulsa for the care and treatment of the wounded. Especially should it be noted that the women and men of the First Aid Stations gave voluntary and gratuitous service. While several hundred were given First Aid at the hospitals, the doctors officiating, and the hospitals themselves have presented bills in full for all services rendered, which bills have been paid out of relief funds.

BURNINGS

Thirty-five city blocks were looted systematically, then burned to a cinder, and the ten thousand population thereof scattered like chaff before the wind. All evidence show that most of the houses were burned from the inside. Eye witnesses say that the methods used were, first, to pile bedding, furniture and other burnable material together, then to apply matches. Eye witnesses also claim that many houses were set afire from aeroplanes. (In this connection it should be noted that while many houses and outbuildings in the Greenwood and Fairview Additions were destroyed, other were allowed to remain untouched.)

PROPERTY LOSSES

Property losses including household goods will reach the two million mark. This must be a conservative figure in view of the fact that law suits covering claims of over $4,000,000.00 have been filed up to July 30th.

Newspaper accounts accompanying this report and statements of eye witnesses, give vivid pictures of what happened.

Where were the police?

Where was the fire department?

Why the temporary breakdown of City and County Government?

The accompanying newspaper reports and editorials will help to answer these questions.

STATE TROOPS

State Troops had arrived and had checked the rioting at noon of Wednesday, the Martial law was in effect, with Adjutant General Barrett of the State in charge.

CHAPTER II

RELIEF AND THE RED CROSS

While "Little Africa" was still burning, while ambulances whizzed to the hospitals, while "dead" wagons were carrying off the victims, while refugees were being driven under guard to places of refuge; and the fiendish looting, robbing, and pillaging was still in progress, different scenes were being enacted "up town".

Realizing that an awful calamity was in progress of perpetration, the Red Cross immediately sprung into action. The women mobilized with incredible speed, and before midnight of Wednesday had made sufficient insignias of Red Crosses on a background of white to placard ambulances, motor vehicles, trucks and other conveyances for the transport of nurses, doctors, supplies and relief workers. This insignia was a pass everywhere.

Mayor Evans early in the day, by written communication, designated the Red Cross as the official Relief Agency.

It should be noted here that even before any official request had been made, the Red Cross had be common consent, sprung into action.

IMMEDIATE CARE OF REFUGEES

Simultaneously refugee camps were installed at Convention Hall, McNulty Ball Park, First Baptist Church and the Fair Grounds. Indeed every available church and public building and many private houses were used to house the homeless.

DIVISION OFFICE CALLED

On the afternoon of Thursday, June 3rd, a telephone message to the St. Louis office summoned division help. On Friday morning Assistant Manager, Maurice Willows, arrived in Tulsa and went into immediate consultation with Red Cross Officials, immediately after which a trip of inspection of refugee camps and hospitals was made.

-3-

PUBLIC WELFARE BOARD

It should be noted at this juncture that the Chamber of Commerce and other city organizations had unitedly appointed a Public Welfare Board consisting of seven of the strongest men of the city to temporarily take charge of the appalling situation. This committee was in its first session when the division representative arrived. This committee met with representatives of the Red Cross and unanimously charged the Red Cross with responsibility for relief operations.

FINANCIAL POLICY

The Public Welfare Board announced that Tulsa would not appeal to the outside world for contributions. This announcement was given wide publicity, which policy apparently met with universal approval. It was understood that in view of the many local complications which would inevitably follow leadership to direct and handle the problems of relief. In order to steer clear of local complications, it seemed wise to ask National Headquarters for finances sufficient to cover such personnel. This contribution was acceptable to the Welfare Board and the local Red Cross officials.

Consequently, on the night of Friday, June 4th, a telegram was dispatched to the Division Manager, which brought forth the cooperation and funds asked for.

ORGANIZATION

Immediate steps were taken to centralize the work of relief which was being done at many different points in the "up town" section, notably the Y.M.C.A., the First Baptist Church and the Red Cross office, 4th and Cincinnati. The Booker Washington School property situated in the heart of the burned area was selected, and by Saturday afternoon all relief operations with the exception of the refugee camps were directed from central headquarters. The following organization was announced on Saturday:

RED CROSS DISASTER RELIEF

General Headquarters and Relief Depot, Booker Washington School

Refugee Camp, Free Fair Grounds, N. R. Graham, Director.

Emergency Hospital, 510 North Main Street.

Red Cross Home Service (ex-soldiers) 4th & Cincinnati

Tubercular Clinic for whites, 15 West Eleventh St.

ORGANIZATION

Chairman of Local Chapter, Clark Field.

Director of Relief, Maurice Willows.

Assistant L. C. Murray

Registration Bureau: This department has all telegrams and mail, and furnished information about lost relatives.

For tents and bedding apply at the north unit building, Booker Washington School.

For lost or stolen property, apply at 703 East Archer, Mr. Doering.

Clothing Department, Second floor, main building.

For employment apply to N. A. Thompson, first floor, main building.

For nursing service, Miss MacKay; for treatment apply first floor, main building.

Purchasing Department, O. V. Borden, first floor main Bldg.

General Dispensary and Clinic (Negro tubercular, venereal and dental clinics, medical dispensary), unit building at north end fair grounds.

Food Supply, Mrs. Wheeler, first floor Main Bldg.

Motor Transportation Department, first floor Main Bldg. J. C. Anthony.

Director of Relief Depot, J. T. Forster, Mr. Murray's office.

TELEPHONES

Main Headquarters in Relief Depot　　　　　　Cedar 2300

Fair Grounds, Cedar 2509

Commissaries, Osage 6158

Fourth & Cincinnati,   Osage 1772

Emergency Hospital,   Osage 2128

Reconstruction Camp, Cedar 2508

Volunteer workers please report at Fourth & Cincinnati for pass.

Report location of stolen goods and names of culprits to J. M. Adkinson, City Hall.

FAMILY WORK PERSONNEL

During the first days of emergency work the use of many volunteers was imperative. The first person of training or experience to arrive was Mrs. L. V. Watkins, formerly Home Service Secretary of Fort Scott, Kansas. Mrs. Watkins was placed in charge of the registration bureau, where she was ably assisted by Mr. Louis Lefko, Secretary of the Better Business Bureau, Mrs. J. M. Reed, Mr. C. D. Adams, and Mrs. T. L. Golay. A wired request for additional personnel was sent to the Division Office, and after a delay of ten days our family work forces were supplemented by Miss Jean Prout of Memphis, Tenn., Miss Mary Porter Scott of St. Louis, and a little later by Mr. Clarence Dawson of Chicago, Miss Ada Palmer of Chicago, Miss Margaret Williams of St. Louis, and Miss Dorothy Davis of Houston, Texas. The last three remained in Tulsa for a period of days days only. Later the Division office sent Mrs. C. B. MacCartney and Mrs. Gretchen Abbott. These workers were all supplied out of Division funds.

MASS WORK

For the first ten days practically all relief work was conducted mass fashion. The refugee camp at the Fair Ground had been well equipped with plumbing, a refrigerator system, a temporary hospital and first aid stations. Over 2,000 people were housed and fed there, under the supervision of Mr. Newt Graham, and a corps of volunteer assistants.

An additional 2,000 were fed and housed at the Booker T. Washington School properties, while the balance of the refugees were hastily housed in tents, surrounding the Booker T. Washington School. These first relief operations involved the watering and sewering of both camps, making both properties sanitary. In these operations full and ample assistance was rendered by the National Guard and the City of Tulsa. It should be noted that the disaster had wiped out practically every resource that the negroes formerly had. All relief to able-bodied men was given in the form of work, at a wage rate of 25 cents per hour. The men were paid at the end of each day. There were, however, no boarding houses, lunch stands or grocery stores from which to obtain food. This food was supplied to the people at the rate of 20 cents per meal, until the time when temporary lunch stands were erected. In the meantime, the women and children were fed at the Red Cross kitchens.

FAMILY SURVEY

As soon as practical a survey was made to determine family conditions. This operation required one week of time on the part of the family workers. It was found that only a partial survey was possible because of the fact that thousands of negroes had left the city, for parts unknown, and other hundreds were herded together in servants quarters throughout the city. A total of 1765 families were registered. There were 5366 persons in these families, 1620 of which were children under 14 years of age.

It was found that 1115 families had their homes burned, and an additional 314 houses had been looted which were not burned. It was also found that 563 families were crowded into small quarters with other families. (See Supplementary Report)

By the time this survey was completed 184 families had been provided with tent homes, with floors and sides of lumber. An additional 200 tents are being equipped. It should be noted that accurate figures regarding families are difficult to secure, because of the fact that when the disaster occurred people were scattered in every direction. There are parts of families being found as far as Chicago on the north and Houston, Texas on the south. In fact, we have located parts of Tulsa families as far west as Los Angeles.

During the first week following the riot railroad transportation was provided for over 300 people. These were mostly women and children, who were sent to relatives in other parts, with the permission of the localities to which they were sent.

PRESENT RELIEF PROGRAM

It has been generally agreed that the Red Cross will have functioned when all the homeless are provided with shelter, laundry, and cooking outfits and stoves; when the families are reunited as far as possible; when the destitute women and orphaned children are cared for, and those who are able-bodied are placed on a self-supporting basis. (See Supplementary Report.)

RECONSTRUCTION

The problem of reconstruction will be dealt with in another chapter, suffice to say here that the Red Cross had refused to involve itself with the problem of rebuilding a new colored district. This is a task of the city administration.

1921 Tulsa Race Riot "Angels of Mercy"

HOSPITALIZATION, NURSING, AND MEDICAL CARE

There are no public hospitals in Tulsa, there is no tubercular sanitarium. Consequently, during the riot the wounded and sick were taken to the private hospitals, where they were crowded into every available space and given surgical and medical attention. When the private hospitals became over crowded, a large residence was commandeered and equipped. With incredible speed a hospital staff of doctors and nurses were mustered in. 163 operation were performed during the first week, 62 of these being major ones. At the end of two weeks the
Red Cross had equipped four large hospital wards in the Booker T. Washington school house for hospital uses, and all of their patients were transferred to this central hospital.

FIRST AID FOR THE INJURED

Following the riot the Red Cross established a first aid station with Mrs. Clark Fields and a staff of nurses in charge. 531 patients were given first aid care, during the first ten days.

A general dispensary was equipped by the Red Cross in one of the rooms at the Booker Washington School and turned over to the Tulsa County Public Health Association in charge of Miss Richardson and her staff.

A V.D. Clinic was also equipped and operated by the Dr. C. L. Reeder, County Health Physician.

NURSING SURVEY

Immediately following the riot all medical nursing and hospital activities were placed under the supervision of Miss Rosalind MacKay, State Supervisor of Red Cross Nursing. She was ably assisted by Mrs. W. D. Godfrey of the Tulsa Red Cross and Miss Bessie Richardson of the Tulsa County Health Association. The following Red Cross Nurses gave their services for two weeks:

Miss Miser	Tulsa, Okla.
Mrs. Cleveland	Cleveland, Okla.
Mrs. Tosh	Sapulpa, Okla.
Miss Weaver	Osage, Okla.
Miss Thomas	Oklahoma City, Okla.
Miss Swanson	Tulsa, Okla.
Miss Hatch	Tulsa, Okla.
Miss Robinson	Tulsa, Okla.
Miss Trotter	Tulsa, Okla.
Mrs. Watson	Tulsa, Okla.

The most important phase of the work of the nurses was the survey made, with the following results:

Number calls made by Public Health Nurses	4512
Number of patients needing medical or nursing care	531
Classified as follows:	
Maternity	38
Infant Welfare	359
General	154
Sent to Dispensary for treatment	80
Number of Emergency Calls by nurses	84
Nursing care given to our patients	169

VACCINATION

Early in the day the utmost precautions were taken to prevent disease. There were seven cases of smallpox reported at the Fair Grounds before the refugees could be vaccinated. There was some delay in medical organization because of conflict in jurisdiction between the county and city physicians. It was necessary to corral all vaccine and typhoid serum in the state of Oklahoma. Approximately 1800 refugees were vaccinated and treated with serum. There has been no outbreak of disease thus far. The doctors of the city took charge of the health situation through a committee composed of Doctor C. L. Reeder, Doctor H. T. Price, and Doctor R. V. Smith, with Doctor Smith as Chairman. In addition to this committee, Doctor Presson, City Health Physician exercised his functions as sanitarian.

SUMMARY

Chronologically the medical and nursing phase of the relief work was as follows:

1. Immediate surgical and medical care of the wounded at six private hospitals.

2. The mobilization of all available nurses for hospital and field service.

3. Placing the State Supervisor of the Red Cross Nursing in charge.

4. The organization of a committee of doctors under whose direction the state supervisor was to supervise.

5. The mobilization of vaccine and the typhoid serum and the administering of same to the refugees.

6. A Field Survey by Public Health Nurses.

7. The equipping of a First Aid Station, a general dispensary and a V. D. Clinic.

8. Equipping and furnishing a central hospital.

9. The evacuation of the private hospitals.

After one month of service all that is left for the Red Cross to continue is the management and supervision of the central hospital and this will be turned over to Tulsa County when they are in a position to take it over. At the end of five weeks there are still 38 patients in the hospital. Practically all of these are fractures, gunshot wounds and amputations. The Medical and Nursing care to is given by white nurses and white doctors.

STATUS OF WHITES WOUNDED

Our files contain the names of 48 whites who have passed through the hospitals. The greatest secrecy has surrounded the status of these whites, probably for the reason that they do not wish to have their names among those involved in the riot. All of the whites needing Red Cross assistance have been handled by Mrs. Jennie Beam, Secretary of the local Chapter, with headquarters at 4th and Cincinnati Streets. The best information obtainable is contained in a statement rendered by a local private hospital where practically all of the white wounded were given attention. On attempting to check up the hospital bills for payment, it was found that there were an unknown number who were wounded, given First Aid treatment at hospitals and sent directly to their homes. A reasonably accurate checking up of white wounded will be made possible as soon as claims for hospitalization and medical attention are presented. All applications for assistance coming from whites have been referred to Mrs. Jennie Beam at Red Cross Headquarters.

CHAPTER III

FINANCES

This chapter in its beginnings harks back to the commitments of the Public Welfare Board which amounted to, "Go ahead and take care of the relief as it should be done and we will finance all Red Cross needs." The Red Cross proceeded full speed ahead. The Public Welfare Board started a campaign for funds, collecting the sum of $26,000.00 during the first few days. The Welfare Board had also received the promise from the County Commissioners

-10-

of a fund amounting to $60,000, to be made available for Red Cross uses. Immediately after July 1st pending the time when this $60,000 would be available, 25 men had agreed to underwrite the Red Cross for $25,000.

Plans were also underway whereby the Welfare Board was to engineer a rehabilitation and housing program. They expected to raise immediately a sum of $100,000 to start with.

When everything was running smoothly, like a thunderclap out of a clear sky the Mayor of the city, T. D. Evans, declared the Welfare Board out of commission, and in its place appointed a new committee of seven which he called "The Reconstruction Committee".

Thus, the backbone of financial support had been broken, most abruptly. The old Public Welfare Board resigned office at a mass meeting and at the time of their resignation recommitted itself collectively and individually to stand by the Red Cross in financing its relief operations.

The Red Cross therefore was placed in a position of having to deal with a new Reconstruction Committee. It was understood, at first, that the new committee was to function as the agent of the city in the same manner as the old committee. Time, however, has proven that the new committee is politically constituted and is chiefly interested in maneuvering for the transfer of negro properties and the establishment of a new negro district.

When it became apparent that the Reconstruction Committee was powerless to raise funds, the old committee members together with the Chairman Fields of the Red Cross brought about a meeting of the County Commissioners and the Mayor.

The Mayor and Chairman Fields requested the County to allow the local Humane Society to relieve the Red Cross of its work. The County Commissioners, however, went into reverse and suggested to the Mayor that the Red Cross was the only organization competent to deal with the relief situation. The commissioners and the Excise Board forcefully suggested that the Mayor include $40,000 from the 1921 City Budget to be used by the Red Cross, in finishing its relief program. The Mayor promptly acceded.

This leaves the financial status as follows:

Appropriation from County of Tulsa	$ 60,000.00
Appropriation from City of Tulsa	40,000.00
Private Donations to Relief Fund	24,865.36
Merchandise Contributions	6,000.00
	$130,865.36

Of this amount approximately $24,577.31 has been expended, in addition to the $6,000.00 in merchandise contributions which have been used, or a total of $30,577.31. (See Supplementary Report for new figures.)

PROGRAM FOR IMMEDIATE FUTURE

The Red Cross relief program must carry through to a point where these destitute, homeless, and sick people can be adjusted into new homes, hospitals, or given over to the care of local agencies. It should be indicated in this report that there is in Tulsa no modern, record keeping, case-work agency dealing with dependent families. There are no public hospitals nor facilities. Prior to the fire there was a small private negro hospital and a general dispensary for colored people, both of which were burned.

It should also be indicated most clearly that the County Commissioners, the City Authorities, the white population and the negroes themselves, insist that the Red Cross shall carry on until completion, that part of the work which can be considered "temporary relief".

RECONSTRUCTION

All that has been said in this report has had to do with emergency and temporary relief. Two months have elapsed since the trouble started, and on this date, July 31st, no rehabilitation nor practical reconstruction program has been outlined by the city government.

Early in the day the Red Cross made it clear that it was not its function to engineer plans for the acquisition of a new residence district, nor for converting any portion of the burned area into a commercial wholesale or industrial district. It was recognized at once, however, that the most suitable action, from a civic and business standpoint, would be the acquisition of that part of the burned area bordering on the railroad tracks, for future industrial or commercial expansion. Public opinion seems in favor of this general proposition. Any such plan, however, it has been pointed out would involve (1) the organization of a Housing Corporation or Holding Company which would act for the municipality in appraising and purchasing from the negro property owners their holdings; (2) the raising of sufficient funds to back the enterprise; (3) the acquiring of a new residential district to be sewered, watered, and lighted; (4) a committee or sub-committee to help the negroes clear up their property equities and to assist them in re-purchasing and rebuilding.

The above general suggestions were, on June 4th, made to the representatives of the Public Welfare Board in session at the City Hall. This board concurred and Chairman L. J. Martin outlined in writing a plan which would virtually embody the above suggestions. All that was necessary for the first plans, which among other things included plans for sufficient funds to start the enterprise immediately. It was well known in this connection that several men connected with the Public Welfare Board had agreed to liberally finance the move.

MAYOR EVANS SPILLS THE BEANS

A close reading of the newspaper articles in this report will show that just at the time when the Welfare Board was ready to announce its plans to the public, Mayor Evans again took up the reins of positive authority at the head of the city government. His first act was to discharge the old Public Welfare Board. He immediately appointed a new committee which he named the "The Reconstruction Committee". This new committee was politically constituted and did not have in its membership men of large financial power or influence. Later on this committee membership was enlarged sufficiently to include representatives from the banking interests. Seven weeks have elapsed at present writing. The Reconstruction Committee has shown practically nothing in the way of definite results.

Because of the many complications, political and otherwise, the Red Cross is steering clear of the so-called reconstruction processes which engage the City Hall authorities.

EXTENSION OF FIRE LIMITS

One of the first acts was to extend the fire limits to embrace practically all of the burned area. This move automatically made it impossible for the rebuilding of frame houses on the old properties. Shortly after this action the Red Cross asked the city authorities to grant the negroes permission to build temporary wooden houses on their lots. This permission was granted, only to be recalled a week later when it was found that a startling number of houses were under erection within the newly-extended fire limits. Thus, at present writing, little, if any progress is being made in re-building in the burned district. We advise the reading of the attached newspaper clippings, which give reports from the Reconstruction Committee. Summarized, their activities revolve around the erection of a public sentiment which would force the negroes to rebuild in a section somewhere outside the city limits. Concurrently, it was hoped that public opinion would become sufficiently strong in favor of a Union Station site or a Commercial District, to bring about the financing of some such project. The Committee has not, however, evolved or stated any practical plan of accomplishment.

THE NEGRO ATTITUDE

The negroes have consistently said to the City, "Pay us for what we have lost and we will talk to you about selling what we have left." It is entirely safe to say that the rebuilding situation is still unsettled and chaotic. Neither the city nor the negroes know what to do nor what will come next.

CONTINUED RELIEF

In the meantime, the Red Cross has been pressed to the limit in placing the negroes on a living and self-supporting basis, in caring for the sick, and in assisting in disease prevention.

-13-

THE RED CROSS RELATIONSHIPS

The Tulsa County Chapter, with the guidance of the Division Representative, is responsible for the Red Cross policy execution. The workers from the Division Office have been supplied the local chapter at Division expense. Altho using funds from the public treasury it maintains an independent position, in the handling of such funds.

The accounting system is under general supervision of the Division Accountant.

ADDENDA

The newspaper clippings and pictures tell the rest of the story. All local persons contributing valuable services are mentioned in these articles. Be it said, however, in this report that the Red Cross has had the united support and good will of the whole population, all political factions and both of the newspapers.

It has been taken for granted that the Red Cross is the only organization which could minister to both blacks and whites and maintain a strictly neutral position on all political and racial questions.

Respectfully submitted,

(signed)   Maurice Willows, Director.

R E P O R T

By Maurice Willows

1921 Tulsa Race Riot *"Angels of Mercy"*

TULSA COUNTY CHAPTER AMERICAN RED

CROSS DISASTER RELIEF COMMITTEE

PREFACE

The story of the tragedy enacted in Tulsa, Okla. on the night of May 31st, 1921, and the morning of June 1st, 1921, has been told and retold in the press of the country, with all sorts of variations as to causes, actual happenings and immediate results.

The unprejudiced and indirectly interested people have from the beginning referred to the affair as the "race riot", others with deeper feeling refer to it as a "massacre", while many who would saddle the blame upon the negro, have used the designation, "artfully coined", "negro up rising". After six months work among them, it has been found the majority of the negroes who were the greatest sufferers refer to June 1st, 1921, as "the time of dewa'". Whatever people choose to call it the word or phase has not yet been coined which can adequately describe the events of June 1st last.

This report refers to the tragedy as a "disaster".

(Signed)

Director.

1921 Tulsa Race Riot "Angels of Mercy"

NARRATIVE REPORT AS OF DECEMBER 31ST, 1921.

CHAPTER 1

The real truth regarding the underlying causes of the short-lived civil war which turned Tulsa, Oklahoma, into a bedlam on the morning of June 1st, 1921, may come to the surface in the future. The consensus of opinion, after six months intervening time, places the blame upon "the lack of law enforcement".

"Race Riot" it has been most generally termed, yet whites were killed and wounded by whites in the protection of white property against the violence of the white mob. The elements of race rioting were present, from all evidences, on the night of May 31st, but the wholesale destruction of property - life and limb, in that section of the city occupied by negroes on June 1st between the hours of daylight and noon, testifies to a one-sided battle.

Altho newspaper clipping attached indicates the apparent local cause of the trouble, subsequent developments have proven that the arrest of the negro boy was merely an incident. Both the negro boy and girl have dropped out of the picture, it being shown that there was no grounds for any prosecution of the boy.

Those persons desiring to satisfy themselves as to causes, are respectfully referred to newspaper accounts of the trial of the Chief of Police, which are contained in this volume.

It should be noted, however, that while the original shooting took place at the County Jail on the night of May 31st, the actual burning, pillaging, and destruction was consummated during the daylight hours of June 1st in the district nearly a mile from the Court House.

All that fire, rifles, revolvers, shot guns, machine guns, and organized inhuman passion could do with thirty-five blocks with its twelve thousand negro population, was done.

Those interested in details bearing on locations, methods used, and the organization of the mobs, both black and white, should refer to newspaper accounts contained herewith.

DEAD

The number of dead is a matter of conjecture. Some knowing ones estimate the number of killed as high as 300, others estimates being as low as 55. The bodies were hurriedly rushed to burial, and the records of many burials are not to be found. For obvious reasons this report cannot deal with this subject.

INJURED

One hundred and eight-four negroes and forty-eight whites were in hospitals for surgical care as charges of the Red Cross, within twenty-four hours after the disaster. Five hundred and thirty-one were given First Aid at the Red Cross Stations during the first three days.

An adequate picture of conditions relating to the injured cannot be written. Eye witnesses will long remember the speeding ambulances, the crowded hospitals, drugstores, churches, and First Aid Stations. While the records show 763 wounded, this does not include wounded people afterwards found on practically all roads leading out of Tulsa. Wounded people turned up at Muskogee, Sapulpa, and other adjourning towns, and as far north as Kansas City. Neither do records tell of the after-the-riot developments. The Red Cross records show eight definite cases of premature childbirth which resulted in death of the babies.

Subsequent developments also show that of the maternity cases given attention by Red Cross doctors, practically all have presented complications due to the riot.

1921 Tulsa Race Riot "Angels of Mercy"

Too much credit cannot be given to the white citizens of Tulsa for the care and treatment rendered the wounded. Especially should it be noted that the women and men at the First Aid Stations gave voluntary and gratuitous service. While several hundred were given First Aid at the hospitals free of charge, the hospitals themselves, which were crowded with patients ultimately presented bills in full for all services rendered, which bills have been paid out of relief funds. It should also be made clear that the attending surgeons almost without exception have been paid in full for the services rendered in the emergency.

BURNINGS

Thirty-five city blocks were looted systematically, then burned to a cinder, and the twelve thousand population thereof scattered like chaff before the wind. All evidences show that most of the houses were burned from the inside. Eye witnesses say that the methods used were, first, to pile bedding, furniture and other burnable material together, then to apply matches. Eye witnesses also claim that many houses were set a fire from aeroplanes. (In this connection it should be noted that while many houses and buildings in the Greenwood and Fairview Additions were destroyed, other houses, evidently chosen ones, were allowed to stand untouched. During the months following the disaster the Relief workers have gathered interesting information as to the ownership of the houses were intact.)

PROPERTY LOSSES

Property losses included household goods will easily reach the four million mark. This must be a conservative figure in view of the fact that law suits covering claims of over $4,000,000 were filed up to July 30th. A large number of property owners were not at that time heard from.

Newspaper accounts accompanying this report and statements of eye witnesses, give vivid pictures of what happened.

Where were the police?

Where was the fire department?

Why the temporary breakdown of City and County government?

The accompanying newspaper reports and editorials will help to answer these questions.

STATE TROOPS

State Troops had arrived and had checked the rioting at noon of Wednesday, and Martial Law was in effect, with Adjutant General Barrett of the State in charge.

CHAPTER II

RELIEF AND THE RED CROSS

While "Little Africa" was still burning, while ambulances whizzed to the hospitals, while "dead" wagons were carrying off the victims, while refugees were being driven under guard to places of refuge; and the fiendish looting, robbing, and pillaging was still in progress, different scenes were being enacted "up town".

Realizing that an awful calamity was in progress of perpetration, the Red Cross immediately sprung into action. The women mobilized with incredible speed, and before midnight of Wednesday had made sufficient insignias of Red Crosses on a background of white, to placard ambulances, motor vehicles, trucks and other conveyances for the transport of nurses, doctors, supplies and relief workers. This insignia was a pass everywhere.

Mayor Evans early in the day, by written communication, designated the Red Cross as the official Relief Agency.

It should be noted here that even before any official request has been made, the Red Cross had by common consent, sprung into action.

IMMEDIATE CARE OF REFUGEES

Simultaneously refugee camps were installed at Convention Hall, McNulty Ball Park, First Baptist Church and the Fair Grounds. Indeed every available church and public building and many private homes were used to house the homeless.

DIVISION OFFICE CALLED

On the afternoon of Thursday, June 3rd, a telephone message to the St. Louis office summoned division help. On Friday morning Assistant Manager, Maurice Willows, arrived in Tulsa, and went into immediate consultation with Red Cross officials, immediately after which a trip of inspection of refugee camps and hospitals were made.

PUBLIC WELFARE BOARD

It should be noted at this juncture that the Chamber of Commerce and other city organizations had unitedly appointed a Public Welfare Board consisting of seven of the strongest men of the city to temporarily take charge of the appalling situation. This Committee was in its first session when the Division representative arrived. This committee met with representatives of the Red Cross and unanimously charged the Red Cross with responsibility for relief operations.

FINANCIAL POLICY

The Public Welfare Board announced that Tulsa would not appeal to the outside world

-5-

for contributions. This announcement was given wide publicity, which policy apparently met with universal approval. It was understood that in view of the many local complications which would inevitably follow, that the National Red Cross should be asked to furnish expert leadership to direct and handle the problems of relief. In order to steer clear of local complications it seemed wise to ask National Headquarters for finances sufficient to cover such personnel. This contribution was acceptable to the Welfare Board and the local Red Cross officials.

Consequently, on the night of Friday, June 4th, a telegram was dispatched to the Division Manager, which brought forth the cooperation and funds asked for.

ORGANIZATION

Immediate steps were taken to centralize the work of relief which was being done at many different points in the "up town" section, notably the Y.M.C.A., the First Baptist Church and the Red Cross office at 4th and Cincinnati. The Booker Washington School property situated in the heart of the burned area was selected, and by Saturday afternoon all relief operations with the exception of the refugee camps were directed from central headquarters. The following organization was announced on Saturday:

RED CROSS DISASTER RELIEF

General Headquarters and Relief Depot, Booker Washington School.

Refugee Camp, Free Fair Grounds, N. R. Graham, Director.

Emergency Hospital, 510 North Main Street.

Red Cross Home Service (ex-soldiers) 4th & Cincinnati.

Tubercular Clinic for whites, 15 West Eleventh St.

1921 Tulsa Race Riot "Angels of Mercy"

ORGANIZATION

Acting Chairman of Local Chapter, Clark Field.

Director of Relief, Maurice Willows.

Assistant L. C. Murray.

Registration Bureau: This department handled all telegrams and mail, and furnished information about lost relatives.

"For tents and bedding apply at the north unit building, Booker Washington School."

"For lost or stolen property, apply at 703 East Archer, Mr. Doering."

Clothing Department, Second floor, main building.

"For employment apply at N. A. Thompson, first floor, main building".

"For nursing service, Miss MacKay; for treatment apply first floor, main building."

Purchasing Department, O. V. Borden, first floor main Bldg.

General Dispensary and Clinic (Negro tubercular, venereal and dental clinics, medical dispensary), unit building at north end fair grounds.

Food Supply, Mrs. Wheeler, first floor Main Bldg.

Motor Transportation Department, first floor main building, J. C. Anthony.

Director of Relief Depot, J. T. Forster, Mr. Murray's office.

TELEPHONES

Main Headquarters in Relief Depot.	Cedar 2300
Fair Grounds.	Cedar 2509
Commissaries.	Cedar 6158
Fourth & Cincinnati	Osage 1772

1921 Tulsa Race Riot "Angels of Mercy"

    Emergency Hospital -   -   -   Cedar 2128

    Reconstruction Camp.-   -   -   Cedar 2508

Volunteer workers please report at Fourth & Cincinnati for pass.

Report location of stolen goods and names of culprits to J. M. Adkinson, City Hall.

FAMILY WORK PERSONNEL

During the first days of emergency work the use of many volunteers was imperative. The first person of training or experience to arrive was Mrs. L. V. Watkins, formerly Home Service Secretary at Fort Scott, Kansas. Mrs. Watkins was placed in charge of the registration bureau, where she was ably assisted by Mr. Louis Lefko, Secretary of the Better Business Bureau, Mrs. J. M. Reed, Mr. C. D. Adams, and Mrs. T. L. Goley. A wired request for additional personnel was sent to the Division Office, and after a delay of ten days our family work forces were supplemented by Miss Jean Prout of Memphis, Tennessee, Miss Mary Porter Scott of St. Louis, and a little later by Mr. Clarence Dawson of Chicago, Miss Ada Palmer of Chicago, Miss Margaret Williams of St. Louis, and Miss Dorothy Davis of Houston, Texas. The last three remained in Tulsa for a period of ten days only. Later the Division Office sent Mrs. C. B. MacCartney and Mrs. Gretchen Abbott. These workers were all supplied out of Division Funds.

MASS WORK

For the first ten days practically all relief work was conducted mass fashion. The refugee camp at the Fair Grounds had been well equipped with plumbing, a refrigerator system, a temporary hospital and first aid stations. Over 2,000 people were housed and fed there, under the supervision of Mr. Newt Graham, and a corps of volunteer assistants.

-8-

An additional 2,000 were fed and housed at the Booker T. Washington School properties, while the balance of the refugees were hastily housed in tents, surrounding the Booker T. Washington School. These first relief operations involved the watering and sewering of both camps making both properties sanitary. In these operations full and ample assistance was rendered by the National Guard and the City of Tulsa. It should be noted that the disaster had wiped out practically every resource that the negroes formerly had. All relief to able bodied men was given in the form of work, at a wage rate of 25 cents per hour. The men were paid at the end of each day. There were, however, no boarding houses, lunch stands or grocery stores from which to obtain food. This food was supplied at the rate of 20 cents per meal, until the time when temporary lunch stands were erected. In the meantime, the women and children were fed at the Red Cross kitchens.

FAMILY SURVEY

From time to time as found practicable, house to house surveys have been made to determine the next immediate relief needs of the affected families. From week to week the emergency relief situation has been made according to the needs of the moment. The first survey was necessarily a partial one for the reason that literally thousands of negroes had left the country for parts unknown and other hundreds were crowded together in servants quarters throughout the city. The first survey made during the week following the disaster showed 1765 families in Tulsa more or less seriously affected. There were 5366 persons in these families, 1620 of which were children under fourteen years of age.

As far as figures were obtainable, it was found that 1115 residences have been destroyed exclusive of stores, cafes, and other business properties. It was ascertained that in addition,

314 residences had been looted of practically all household possessions and valuables, which houses were not burned. It was also found that 563 families were crowded into small quarters with other families.

No accurate estimate was possible on the number of refugees that left the district during and immediately following the trouble. As a basis of calculations, after seven months of relief work, it is noted that a total of 2480 family case records have been opened, indicating that at least 715 families temporarily left Tulsa, returning later for various reasons. All evidences show that most of the families returned to their old homes after the cotton picking season was over, in order to place their children in school and to reestablish where possible their old homes.

There is little indication that other cities were seriously burdened with Tulsa dependents. Indications also point to the fact that the majority of these families found employment for themselves and children in the agricultural districts.

HOUSING MEASURES

During the week of the riot, 284 army tents, 16 x 16, with a few, 17 x 21, had been thrown up to accommodate the refugees. The provisions, however, did not meet the conjected conditions in servants quarters.

By June 18th, 184 of those tents had been provided with floors and sides of lumber, wire screening and screen doors. Housing measures were handicapped because of insufficient sanitation and because of the lack of sewerage and also of the impossibility of inducing the city authorities to quickly furnish enough sanitary toilets.

HEALTH

With every sanitary condition unfavorable, thru one device or another, typhoid and other epidemics were avoided. In many instances strict measures were taken to segregate a few of the worst cases of typhoid, and the liberal use of typhoid serum, together with lime and other disinfectants, played a part in this epidemic.

GENERAL RELIEF PROGRAM

In the early days it was generally agreed that the Red Cross would have functioned when the homeless were provided with shelter, laundry outfits, cooking outfits and stoves; when sufficient, simple, plain bedding was provided; when the families were reunited as far as possible; when the destitute women and children were cared for; and when the able-bodied were placed on a self-supporting basis.

RECONSTRUCTION

The problem of reconstruction will be dealt with elsewhere. Suffice it to say that the Red Cross has refused to involve itself with the problem of permanent reconstruction or the rebuilding of a new colored district. This obviously was a task for the city and county administrations.

The uninformed should know that approximately two thirds of the burned area is located beyond the city limits.

HOSPITALIZATION, NURSING AND MEDICAL CARE

There are no public hospitals in Tulsa, there is no tubercular sanitarium. Consequently, during the riot the wounded and sick were taken to the private hospitals, where they were crowded into every available space and given surgical and medical attention. When the private hospitals became over crowded, a large residence was commandeered and equipped. With incredible speed a hospital staff of doctors and nurses were mustered in. 163 operations were performed during the first week, 82 of these being major ones. At the end of two weeks the Red Cross had equipped four large hospital wards in the Booker T. Washington school house for hospital uses, and all of the patients were transferred to his central hospital.

FIRST AID FOR THE INJURED

Following the riot the Red Cross established a first aid station with Mrs. Clark Fields and a staff of nurses in charge. 531 patients were given first aid care, during the first ten days.

A general dispensary was equipped by the Red Cross in one of the rooms at the Booker Washington School and turned over to the Tulsa County Public Health Association in charge of Miss Richardson and her staff.

A V. D. Clinic was equipped also and operated by the Red Cross and turned over to Mr. C. L. Reeder, County Health Physician.

NURSING SURVEY

Immediately following the riot all medical, nursing and hospital activities were placed under the supervision of Miss Rosalind MacKay, State Supervisor of Red Cross nursing. She was ably assisted by Mrs. W. D. Godfrey of the Tulsa Red Cross and Miss Donnie Richardson of the Tulsa County Health Association. The following Red Cross Nurses gave their services for two weeks:

Miss Miser	--	Tulsa, Okla.
Mrs. Cleveland	--	Cleveland, Okla.
Mrs. Tosh	--	Sapulpa, Okla.
Miss Weaver	--	Osage, Okla.
Miss Thomas	--	Oklahoma City, Okla.

Miss Swanson	--	Tulsa, Okla.
Miss Hatch	--	Tulsa, Okla.
Miss Robinson	--	Tulsa, Okla.
Miss Trotter	--	Tulsa, Okla.
Mrs. Watson	--	Tulsa, Okla.

The most important phase of the work of the nurses was the house to house survey made, with the following results:

Number calls made by Public Health Nurses	-	4512.
Number of patients needing medical or nursing care-	-	551
Classified as follows:		
Maternity	-	38
Infant Welfare	-	359
General	-	154
Sent to Dispensary for treatment	-	80
Number emergency calls by nurses	-	84
Nursing care given to out patients	-	169

VACCINATION

Early in the day the utmost precautions were taken to prevent disease. There were seven cases of small pox reported at the Fair Grounds before the refugees could be vaccinated. There was some delay in medical organization because of conflict in jurisdiction between the county and city physicians. It was necessary to corral all vaccine and typhoid serum in the state of Oklahoma. Approximately 1800 refugees were vaccinated and treated with the serum. The doctors of the city took charge of the health situation through a committee composed of Doctors C. L. Reader, H. T. Price, and R. V. Smith, with Dr. Smith as Chairman. In addition to this committee, Doctor Presson, City Health Physician, exercised his functions as sanitarian.

SUMMARY

Chronologically the medical and nursing phase of the relief work was as follows:

1. Immediate surgical and medical care of the wounded at six private hospitals.

2. The mobilization of all available nurses for hospital and field service.

3. Placing the State Supervisor of the Red Cross Nursing in charge.

4. The organization of a committee of doctors under whose direction the state supervisor was to supervise.

5. The mobilization of vaccine and the typhoid serum and the administering of same to the refugees.

6. A Field Survey by Public Health Nurses.

7. The equipping of a First Aid Station, a general dispensary, and a V.D. Clinic.

8. Equipping and furnishing a central hospital.

9. The evacuation of the private hospitals.

10. The building of a suitable hospital for the more permanent care of those wounded during the disaster and all of the sick needing hospitalization because of the lack of suitable homes. An arrangement was made whereby the County Commissioners and the Board of Education jointly turned over for Red Cross uses certain properties located at 324 North Hartford. On this centrally located site a nine-room hospital building was erected, the Red Cross furnishing the building material and the East End Relief Committee (colored) furnished the labor. This made the hospital a cooperative enterprise. The property when built represented an investment of approximately $68,000.

11. The evacuation of the Booker Washington School property as relief and hospital

headquarters on September 1st, 1921.

12. The formation of a Colored Hospital Association, which is incorporated under State Law. The purpose of this Association is to take over the management of this hospital and to ultimately take title to the same. A full statistical report of hospital operations is given elsewhere.

To the everlasting credit of Tulsa and the Red Cross, it should be said that the very best surgical and medical care obtainable has been given the negro patients. Dr. H. S. Browne (white) has supervised the medical and nursing service since the first week following the disaster. A white nursing staff was maintained until the Colored Hospital Association began functioning, January 1st, 1922.

STATUS OF WHITES' WOUNDED

Our files contain the names of 48 whites who have passed through the hospitals. The greatest secrecy has surrounded the status of these whites, probably for the reason that they do not wish to have their names among those involved in the rioting. All of the whites needing Red Cross assistance have been handled by Mrs. Jennie K. Beam, Secretary of the Local Chapter, with headquarters at 4th and Cincinnati Streets. The best information obtainable is contained in a statement rendered by a local private hospital where practically all of the whites wounded were given attention. On attempting to check the hospital bills for payment it was found that there were an unknown number who were wounded, given First Aid treatment at hospitals and sent directly to their homes. The number of whites wounded probably exceeded the number given in this record, as the figures given represent the cases whose medical care was actually paid for out of relief funds. (Many humorous instances might be cited of claims

-15-

presented by "innocent bystanders" for the payment of doctors' bills). All such claims were rigidly investigated and many were turned down for the reason that it could not be shown that the wounded parties were "innocent bystanders", or persons in the employ of the city or county for guard purposes. Quite early in the fall, a claim for $85.00, doctor bill, was presented by a young white man for gunshot wound treatment. The claim was of the "innocent bystander" kind. After lengthy explanation on the part of the claimant as to how the injury was incurred, but after his admission that he was not employed by the city or county, the Red Cross record-keeper confronted him with a full sized photograph of the same young man in the middle of the riot district with a shot gun over his shoulder and high powered rifle in his hand. Altho he did not deny the identity, he has not been seen at the Red Cross office since. After this experience, no further claims have been made by "innocent bystanders".

FINANCES

This chapter in its beginnings harks back to the commitments of the Public Welfare Board which amounted to, "Go ahead and take care of the relief as it should be done and we will finance all Red Cross needs." The Red Cross preceded full speed ahead. The Public Welfare Board started a campaign for funds, collecting the sum of $26,000.00 during the few days at first. The Welfare Board had also received the promise from the County Commissioners of a fund amounting to $60,000.00, to be made available for Red Cross uses. Immediately after July 1st pending the time when this $60,000.00 would be available, 25 men had agreed to underwrite the Red Cross for $25,000.00.

Plans were also underway whereby the Welfare Board was to engineer a rehabilitation and housing program. They expected to raise immediately a sum of $100,000 to start with.

When everything was running smoothly, like a thunderclap out of a clear sky the Mayor of the City, T. E. Evans, declared the Welfare Board out of commission, and in its place appointed a new committee of seven which he called "The Reconstruction Committee".

Thus, the backbone of financial support had been broken, most abruptly. The original Public Welfare Board resigned office at a mass meeting and at the time of their resignation recommitted itself collectively and individually to stand by the Red Cross Relief Committee if their services should be necessary.

The Red Cross therefore was placed in a position of having to deal with a new Reconstruction Committee. It was understood, at first, that the new committee was to function as the agent of the city in the same manner as the old committee. Time, however, has proven that the new committee was politically constituted and was chiefly interest in maneuvering for the transfer of negro property and the establishment of a new negro district.

When it became apparent that the Reconstruction Committee was powerless to raise funds, the old committee members, together with Chairman Fields of the Red Cross, brought about a meeting of the County Commissioners and the Mayor.

The Mayor and Chairman Fields of the Red Cross Committee requested the County to allow the local Humane Society to relieve the Red Cross of its work. The County Commissioners, however, went into reverse and suggested to the Mayor that the Red Cross was the only organization competent to deal with the relief situation. The Commissioners and the Excise Board forcefully suggested that the Mayor include $40,000.00 in the 1921-1922 budget to be used by the Red Cross, in finishing its relief program. The Mayor promptly and gracefully acceded.

This left the appropriation status as of September 1st as follows:

Appropriation from County of Tulsa	$60,000.00
Appropriation from City of Tulsa	40,000.00
Private Donations to Relief Fund	24,865.36
Merchandise Contributions	6,000.00
	$130,865.36

The financial report and statement indicates full payment of the appropriation made by the county but a falling down on the part of the city. It should properly be said that there is no indication that the public has been aware of the failure of the city to meet its properly and legally made pledges of financial support. On the other hand there is every indication of disinterestedness and lack of sympathy on the part of certain city officials. It was deemed best by the Relief Committee not to press its claims upon city funds. This meant the curtailment and limitation of the relief program to the extent of $22,400.00. It should be said that the County officials have from the beginning shown a magnanimous spirit toward the stricken colored population, while on the other hand the city officials in control of the municipal policy, certainly for the period ending October 1st, were entirely out of sympathy with the relief program. In fairness to Mayor Evans it should be recorded that since October 1st, or more accurately speaking, since certain court decisions were made restricting the city from interferring in the rebuilding processes, he and other city officials have shown an increased and more sympathetic interest in the condition of the colored people.

PLANS FOR THE WINTER

From month to month as conditions changed and after conference with W. Frank Persons, the Vice-Chairman of the Red Cross, James L. Fieser, Division Manager, and local chapter officials December 1st, 1921, was set as the date for closing the relief operations of the American Red Cross. Certain conditions, however, delayed the closing date to December 31st. The primary reason for this delay in closing, was the lack of any modern, record-keeping, case-work agency dealing with dependent families in Tulsa. There are no public hospitals nor facilities for handling the problems remaining. Prior to the fire there was a small private negro hospital and a general dispensary for colored people, both of which were burned.

It should also be indicated most clearly that the County Commissioners, the City Authorities, the white population and the negroes themselves, insisted upon the Red Cross continuing its relief work thru the winter, but that the best judgement of the Red Cross Relief Committee, Division and National offices, dictated the final decision to close on December 31st, 1921.

Arrangements have been made whereby the "Tulsa Relief Trusteeship" will maintain a nucleus of workers and an office in the colored district to carry on the work of salvage and relief until the same is deemed unnecessary.

RECONSTRUCTION

All that has been said in this report has had to do with emergency and temporary relief. Seven months have elapsed since the trouble started, and on this date, December 31st, no rehabilitation nor practical reconstruction program has been outlined by the city government.

Early in the day the Red Cross made it clear that it was not its function to engineer plans for the acquisition of a new negro district, nor for converting any portion of the burned area into a commercial wholesale or industrial district. It was recognized at once, however, that the most suitable action, from a civic and business standpoint, would be the acquisition of that part of the burned area bordering on the railroad tracks, for future industrial or commercial expansion. Public opinion seemed in favor of this general proposition. Any such plan, however, it was pointed out, would involve, (1) the organization of a Housing Corporation or Holding Company which would act for the municipality in appraising and purchasing from the negro property owners their holdings; (2) the raising of sufficient funds to back the enterprise; (3) the acquiring of a new residential district to be sewered, watered, and lighted; (4) a committee or sub-committee to help the negroes clear up their property equities and to assist them in re-purchasing and rebuilding.

The above general suggestions were, on June 4th, made to the representatives of the Public Welfare Board in session at the City Hall. This board concurred and Chairman L. J. Martin outlined in writing a plan which would virtually embody the above suggestions. All that was necessary for the first plans, which among other things included plans for sufficient funds to start the enterprise immediately. It was well known in this connection that several men connected with the Public Welfare Board had agreed to liberally finance the move.

A CONSTRUCTION PLAN UP SET

A close reading of the newspaper articles in this report will show that just at the time when the Welfare Board was ready to announce its plans to the public, Mayor Evans again took up the reins of positive authority at the head of the city government. His first act was to discharge the old Public Welfare Board. He immediately appointed a new committee which he named "The Reconstruction Committee". This new committee was politically constituted and did not have in its membership men of large financial power or influence. Later on this committee membership was enlarged sufficiently to include representatives from the banking interests. Seven months have elapsed. The so-called Reconstruction Committee has gone out of existence without recording any constructive results.

Because of the many complications, political and otherwise, the Red Cross has successfully steered clear of the so-called "reconstruction processes" which engage the "committee" during the early and late fall.

EXTENSION OF FIRE LIMITS

One of the first acts of the new committee was to extend the fire limits to embrace practically all of the burned area within the city limits. This move automatically made it impossible for the rebuilding of frame houses on the old properties. Shortly after this action, the Red Cross asked the city authorities to grant the negroes permission to build temporary wooden houses on their lots. This permission was granted, only to be recalled a week later when it was found that a startling number of houses were under erection within the newly-extended fire limits. The agitation for and against the permanency of the fire limits proceeded for two months and until the district court - three judges presiding - permanently enjoined the city officials from executing the provisions of the fire ordinance recorded immediately after the fire. During the interim the negroes were prevented from helping themselves by rebuilding. With the final court decision, the so-called Reconstruction Committee automatically went out of business and rebuilding processes began in earnest. The statistical report appended indicates the progress made since that time.

Summarized, the activities revolve around the creation of a public sentiment which would force the negroes to rebuild in a section somewhere outside the city limits.

Concurrently, it was hoped by some that public opinion would become sufficiently strong in favor of a Union Station site or a Commercial District, to bring about the financing of some such project. The Committee did not, however, evolve or state any practical plan for helping the household situation.

THE NEGRO ATTITUDE

The negroes have consistently said to the City, "Pay us for what we have lost and we will talk to you about selling what we have left". The Insurance Companies have consistently refused to honor the payment of insurance moneys because of the riot clause in the insurance policies. No suits for damages have reached the local court dockets and that which has been done is the responsibility of the negroes themselves and their white friends who have stood back of them.

RED CROSS RELATIONSHIPS

The Tulsa County Chapter with the guidance of the Director of Disaster Relief, bore the responsibility for Red Cross policy and execution. The workers from the Division office have been supplied the local chapter at Division expense. Altho using funds from the public treasury, it maintained a strictly independent position in the handling of such funds.

The accounting system has been under general supervision of the Division Accountant and a firm of local Public Accountants.

ADDENDA

The newspaper clippings and pictures tell the rest of the story. All local persons contributing valuable services are mentioned in these articles. Be it said, however, in this report, that the Red Cross has had the united support and good will of the whole population, all political factions and both of the newspapers.

It has been taken for granted that the Red Cross was the only organization which could minister to both blacks and whites and maintain a strictly neutral position on all political and racial questions.

Respectfully submitted.

December 31st, 1921.   Director

FULL   SOCIAL   AND   MEDICAL

RELIEF   REPORT

Up to and including

December 31st, 1921.

1921 Tulsa Race Riot *"Angels of Mercy"*

RELIEF STATISTICS

Total No. families registered	2480
Total No. persons in these families	8624
Total No. detached persons	410
Total No. families with no children	462
Total No. families with no father (missing or dead)	222
Total No. families with no mother (missing or dead)	87
Total houses burned	1256
Total houses looted but not burned	215
Families definitely relieved with clothing, beds, bed clothing, tentage, laundry equipment, cooking utensils, dishes, material for clothing, etc.	1941
Churches housed in Red Cross tents	8
Medicines furnished (outside of hospital)	230
Medical service (in field) given to maternity cases, typhoid cases, and infant cases.	269
Small property adjustments made	88
Transportation furnished (estimated)	475
Telegrams sent or received (relative to riot victims)	1350

RECONSTRUCTION

As of this date, December 30th, 1921, the following list shows progress being made by the negroes in rebuilding in the burned area:

- 180   One-room frame shacks
- 272   Two-room frame shacks
- 312   Three rooms or more, frame
- 1   Large brick church
- 2   Basement Brick Churches
- 4   Frame Churches - one room
- 24   One story brick or cement buildings
- 24   Two story brick or cement buildings
- 3   Three story brick or cement buildings
- 1   Large Theater
- 1   Corrugated Iron Garage
- 2   Filling Stations.

There are still 49 families residing in tent covered houses. All of these are unable to rebuild. The Red Cross has assisted, with the use of funds from the National Association for the Improvement of Colored People, in the erection of 13 homes.

The Red Cross on its own account has transformed 152 tent homes into more or less permanent wooden houses.

FAMILY TASKS YET REMAINING

1. There still remains 49 tent houses to be converted into all wooden ones. While the National Association of Negroes have agreed to cooperate in financing this rebuilding, it is improbable that they will carry out their agreement unless some white guiding hand is present.

2. There is still a number of a hundred families whose destitution is due to the riot still needing constant help of one sort or another.

3. The problems of overcrowding, sufficient bedding and clothing and minor sickness are still present in abundance.

4. The transfer of the hospital has not been completed. A Colored Hospital Association is being incorporated. A staff of colored physicians and nurses are working at the hospital, under the direction of Dr. H. S. Browne and Dr. Butler, but it is too early to throw full responsibility of management and control to the negroes.

    The hospital can and should be made self-sustaining. Wise direction at this time is necessary to insure this.

5. The business end of Red Cross Relief operation cannot close until all December business is closed and the books and accounts audited by public accountants. Such an audit is complete up to September 1st. It is estimated that the final closing accounts will take until January 15th.

SOCIAL RELIEF SUPPLY SCHEDULES

During the first three days following the riot a vast quantity of food was supplied for refugees at the Y.M.C.A., the Fair Grounds, the churches, the Convention Hall, the McNulty Park and other places. Likewise, a vast quantity of bedding supplies, cots, blankets, etc.

These supplies are not listed in the following table, altho these articles were ultimately paid for from relief funds. The cost of these first relief supplies is included in the detailed financial classification.

This supply list is necessarily a partial one, it being impossible to list the endless number of small goods which make up building material, clothing supplies and household equipment. This list does, however, give an idea as to the variety and extent of social relief operations.

Preceeding the list, however, should be the following statement on the methods of distribution.

METHODS OF DISTRIBUTION

Beginning on June 3rd, all family relief supplies given, were incidental to the particular need of a particular family. By a flexible system of family case work each family was encouraged in helping itself to the limit of their ability. Where lumber was donated, for instance, the labor necessary to rebuild or build the tent house was supplied by the family or their negro friends. Exceptions were made only in the cases of widows, sick or helpless people.

Instead of issuing ready-made clothing, cloth was supplied, sewing machines were provided and the raw material turned into clothing by the negro women and girls.

A typical variation was made in the cases of school books for High School pupils. The girls in the High School classes who could not purchase their school books were furnished with work, making hospital garments, nightgowns, underwear, etc., thus enabling them to pay for their books. The High School boys were furnished manual labor, their wages paying for their books.

The same plan was followed with bedding supplies. The raw goods have been furnished power sewing machines have been provided and the women required to manufacture their own quilts, comforts, cot pads, sheets, pillow cases, and pillows.

The following is a list of relief supplies purchased on requisition or donated on invoice as shown:

HOUSING

Article	Purchased	Donated	Made in Workroom	Total
Tents	303	10		313
Lumber	305,160 ft.	72,000 ft.		377,160 ft.
Tent Poles	300			300
Paint	119 gal.			119 gal.
Shingles	41 bun.			41 bun.
Screen Doors	152			152
Screen Wire	16,300 ft.			16,300 ft.
Roofing Paper	125 rolls			125 rolls
Lime	40 bbls.			40 bbls.
Nails	2,233 lbs.			2,233 lbs.

1921 Tulsa Race Riot "Angels of Mercy"

HOUSEHOLD EQUIPMENT

Article	Purchased	Donated	Made in Workroom	Total
Cots	1,222	160		1,382
Blankets	1,491 prs.	225 prs.		1,716 prs.
Comforts	143		360	543
Mattresses	112	36	80	228
Pillows	349		240	589
Cotton Bats	1,540			1,540
Bed Springs	120	16		136
Stoves (cooking)	36	24		60
Stove Piping	1,400 ft.			1,400 ft.
Gas Stoves	54	8		62
Heaters (small)	68			68
Oil Stoves	25	10		35
Lamps	50			50
Chairs	48	26		74
Laundry Tubs	360	16		376
Boilers	360			360
Sets of Irons	350			350
Wash Boards	360			360
Variety Kitchen Utensils	8,272			8,272
Bedsteads	40			40

1921 Tulsa Race Riot *"Angels of Mercy"*

CLOTHING MATERIALS

Article	Purchased	Donated	Made in Workroom	Total
Children's Stockings	500 prs.			500 prs.
Thread	50 doz.			50 doz.
Men's Socks	300 prs.			300 prs.
Women's Stockings	200 prs.			200 prs.

Outing cloth
    (for children's underwear)
Unbleached Domestic
    (underwear)
Ginghams
Cheese Cloth
Denims
Gause for Surgical Dressings
Sheetings   49,982 yds.
Material for Layetts
Quilt Material
Material for aprons
Comfort Material
Diaper Cloth
Dress Cloth
    (Children's School Dresses)

Article	Purchased	Donated	Made in Workroom	Total
Boys' Suits	36			36
Boys' Caps	70			70
Girls Caps	100			100
Children's Shoes	50			50

SCHOOL BOOKS

No. not know. Total cash value of school books furnished. $1,239.00

SUNDRY RELIEF SUPPLIES

Article	Purchased	Donated	Made in Workroom	Total
Disenfectants	24 gal.			24 gal.
Working Tools (spades, wheelbarrows, hammers, saws, shovels, etc.)	204			204

SUNDRY RELIEF SUPPLIES (cont'd)

Article	Purchased	Donated	Made in Workroom	Total
Gas and Water Piping.	2,800 ft.			2,800 ft.

NOTE: Additional information on relief statistics is contained in the financial statement covering expenditures.

SUMMARY OF ACCOMPLISHMENTS

1. During the immediate days after the riot, over four thousand people were housed and fed in detention camps, mass fashion.

2. An unknown number, approximately 2,000, were given shelter and fed wherever houses could be found to accommodate them.

3. Five hospitals were supplied with emergency dressings and medical supplies for care of 183 patients. 521 First Aid cases were cared for at emergency First Aid Stations.

    (Note: It should be noted that all of the hospitals charged their regular fees both for hospital care and surgical attention, the bills being presented to the Red Cross.)

4. Anti-tetanus, typhoid and small-pox serums were administered to over 1,800 people.

5. Hospital care, a general dispensary, a dental clinic, and a V.D. Clinic was equipped and put into service at the Booker T. Washington School and used there until September 1st.

In the meantime a fairly modern nine-roomed hospital has been built ready for occupancy, which was immediately pressed into service on the vacation of the school properties.

6. Over four hundred tent homes were erected with board siding and flooring with screen

doors, these for immediate temporary use.

Since October 1st, two hundred twenty-five of these have been converted into all wood one-room or two-room houses.

7. Over five hundred children, mostly of the lower grades, were furnished school books and many of them school clothes, at the beginning of the school year.

8. During the months of October, November and December, an average of fifteen carpenters were kept at work on daily wages replacing tent homes with wooden shacks. During the same months, an average of fifteen women have been employed in the work room, making underwear, quilts, hospital garments, bedding and clothing equipment.

9. A total of 2480 families have been to the Red Cross office with their troubles. A thorough record of each of these has been made and individual treatment afforded according to the merits of each case. The aim in each instance has been to help the sufferers help themselves, the Red Cross giving material assistance where the needs of the case warranted. In all of these cases the Red Cross workers have acted as counselor and advisors.

CO-OPERATION WITH OTHER AGENCIES

Definite cooperation of the right sort has been given by all local social agencies, the East End Relief Committee, the National Association for the Improvement of the Colored People.

1921 Tulsa Race Riot "Angels of Mercy"

SUMMARY MEDICAL AND SURGICAL RELIEF

No. Wounded Whites Hospitalized During and After Riot at Red Cross Expense.	48
No. Wounded Negroes Hospitalized During and After Riot at Red Cross Expense.	135
No. Negro Cases Hospitalized since Riot.	98
Total Number Persons Receiving Hospital Care.	233
No. Patients Still Remaining In Hospital.	22
Number of Persons Died.	18
No. Persons Who Have From Time to Time Been Discharged	193
No. First Aid Cases During and After Riot	531
No. Colored Physicians Used By Red Cross in Treatment of Sick Since Riot.	11
Total No. of White Physicians Whose Services Were Paid For By the Red Cross	11

Total No. of Nurses Employed By Red Cross During and After the Riot:

a.	Hospital	38	
b.	Field	8	46

Up to and including December 30th, the hospital has been in charge of Dr. H. S. Browne, Attending Physician and Surgeon, and under him a staff of three of the best white nurses obtainable. The white nurses, Mrs. Edmondson, Miss Sizer, and Mrs. Pendergraft, left the service December 28th, the nursing work being taken over by a staff of colored nurses. Dr. H. S. Browne is Supervising Physician and Surgeon.

A Colored Hospital Association has been organized and incorporated to take over the management of the hospital. A staff of colored physicians and surgeons has been organized by Dr. Butler, County Physician, the plan being to have the hospital entirely under the management of the colored people, the property interests for the time being to remain in the hands of the Board of Trustees - three or five white citizens yet to be selected.

1 died December 30th.

1921 Tulsa Race Riot *"Angels of Mercy"*

PATIENTS IN HOSPITAL DEC. 30TH:

1. Cal Arnley - Shot in ankle - old man - may still save leg.

2. Alex Stevenson - Shot in hand - arm and leg - Compound fractures.

Others in Hospital Since Riot:

3. Elsie Walker - 80 yrs old - ulcers in leg - will never be well. Case for County. Homeless.

4. Frank Miller - Old man - T.B. - home burned in riot - case for County.

5. Jake Miller - Old man - suffer paralytic stroke during riot - homeless - case for county.

6. Arthur Morrison - Age 12 - pelegra - homeless since riot - Mother died result injuries in riot.

7. Henry Gamble - Aneurism - may recover - old man - case for County.

8. Charles Carter - T.B. - homeless since riot - case for County Hospital.

Others in Hospital:

9. Charles Caldwell - Hemorrhoids

10. John Williams - Asthma - Syphilitic

11. Richard Ashford - Age 12 - Tumor on Chest.

12. Mary Stewart - Removal Fibroid Tumors, Appendix and Ovaries.

13. Harriet Pierce - Periorphium ovaries, Appendix and Curetment.

14. Bonnie Krout - Infected Jaw.

15. Arthur Montgomery - Shot in Abdomen.

16. Arizona Robinson - Removal of Ovaries and Tumors.

17. Henry Oscar - Pneumonia

18. Mammie Nurse - Tonsils and Throat.

19. Ruth Johnson - Syphilitic - Medical Case.

20. William Collins - Syphilitic

21. Mobeal Adams - T.B. - Case for County

HOSPITAL PERSONNEL

As of December 30th, 1921.

Dr. H. S. Browne and Dr. Butler, white, Supervising Physicians and Surgeons with a staff of negro physicians and surgeons.

Miss Fagg	Day Nurse
Mrs. Marshall	Night Nurse
Mrs. Ragsdale	Asst. Day Nurse
Homer Mosely	Day Orderly
John Grisson	Night Orderly
Rebecca	Nurses Aid
Mrs. Phillips	Cook
Arthur	Asst. Cook

NOTE: Dr. H. S. Browne has consented to remain as Supervisor for a period of fifteen days or as long thereof as may be necessary to turn the patients over to the colored doctors with safety.

SUPPLEMENT TO GENERAL REPORT

JULY 30, 1921.

1921 Tulsa Race Riot *Angels of Mercy*

Tulsa Disaster Relief Statistics

Compiled as of July 31st, 1921

(These records do not show figures for any but those whose records are actually known to the Red Cross office.)

Number of families registered for relief	1912
Number of persons in these families	5739
Number of detached persons	360
Number of families with no children	407
Number of families with no children (missing or dead)	222
Number of families with no mother (missing or dead)	87
Houses burned	1256
Houses looted but no burned	21
Families living in tents at present	245
Families living with other families	649
Families definitely relieved with clothing, beds, bed clothing, tentage, laundry equipment, cooking utensils, dishes, material for clothing, etc.	941
Churches housed in Red Cross tents.	8
Medicines furnished (outside of hospitals)	130
Medical service (in field) given to maternity cases, typhoid cases, and infant cases	69
Small property adjustments made	68
Transportation furnished (estimate)	475
Telegrams sent or received (relative to riot victims)	1250

MEDICAL AND SURGICAL

Hospital cases, definitely charged to Red Cross	183
First Aid cases - during riot	531
Cases still in hospital	32
Maternity cases in hospital awaiting confinement	3
Maternity cases - prospective hospital cases	4

Equipped: 1 general dispensary for Tulsa P.H. Assoc.
              1 V. D. Clinic for County Physician
              1 Dental Clinic
              4 Wards in Hospital

Physicians in Employ of Red Cross ....(colored) 1
                                               ....(white) 1

Total number of nurses employed by Red Cross since riot:
- In hospitals 36
- In field 8
- TOTAL 44
- At present on Staff 5

Number of surgeons whose services were paid for from Red Cross Funds...................... 11

Summary of Accomplishments To Date

1. During the immediate days after the riot, over four thousand people were housed and fed in detention camps, mass fashion.

2. An unknown number, approximately 2,000, were given shelter and fed wherever houses could be found to accommodate them.

3. Five hospitals were supplied with emergency dressings and medical supplies for care of 183 patients. 531 First Aid cases were cared for at emergency First Aid stations.

    > Note: It should be noted that all of the hospitals charged their regular fees both for hospital care and surgical attention - the bills being presented to the Red Cross.

4. Anti-tetanic, typhoid and small-pox serums were administered to over 1,800 people.

    Following the concentration of relief in the Booker T. Washington School, individual work has been done with 1,912 families in addition to many hundreds of detached persons of whom no records were kept. On account of the variety of services rendered, it is impossible to list the kind of services rendered.

5. A modern hospital, general dispensary, dental clinic, and a V. D. Clinic has been equipped and put into service.

6. Over 200 temporary residence tents have been fully equipped with floors, sides, and screens, and the people made as comfortable as possible. 150 women have been supplied with laundry outfits, thus enabling them to partially make a living.

PROBLEMS STILL TO BE MET

1. Of first importance is the evacuation, in late August, of the Booker T. Washington school. This means that our four-ward hospital, the general dispensary, V. D. Clinic, dental clinic, supply rooms, lumber yard, and relief administration offices must find quarters elsewhere.

2. On account of there being no permanent rehabilitation and housing program officially stated or planned, the Red Cross or some other agency must act in a temporary rehabilitation capacity.

    Attention is called to one or two items most important, of which is the preparation of over 1,400 school children for school in September. Probably one-half of these must be furnished from some source or other, clothing, headwear, shoes, stockings, and school equipment.

Next in importance is the probability of a long winter with more sickness than usual, and with no provisions for emergency hospital or nursing care.

I might also call attention to the fact that with fall comes relief needs in bedding which will be stupendous. Practically none of these temporary homes are equipped with stoves, lighting or heating.

It would be insane to argue or assume that more than three-fourths of the negro population are in a position to help themselves - with the more essentials in living without continued assistance. It is quite certain that with the present status of unemployment and reduced wages, with no lessening of the cost of living, that even some wage earners will need emergency assistance.

The solution of these problems cannot be met by a "let alone policy". To avoid chaos among the negroes before spring, these problems must be faced and tackled by the community with sufficient finances and personnel to handle them on a socially sound and economical basis.

A Still Larger Problem

Developments are showing that as the overflow from the old burned district is reaching beyond the city limit, living conditions are becoming worse and worse, especially in the Greenwood addition. Sanitary and sewer arrangements are entirely inadequate and the lack of any policing is fast leading to a probably worse condition than existed before the riot in the old burned area. There is a growing attitude on the part of the city to throw responsibility for moral and sanitary conditions on the County, and the County is unprepared to meet the new condition with the necessary speed.

I might also call attention to the fact that the roads condition leading into the County through the Greenwood section are such in the dry season as to make it a disease-breeding center. Dust and filth accumulates everywhere.

These are but a few of the problems presented for action during the next few months.

1921 Tulsa Race Riot *"Angels of Mercy"*

TULSA AMERICAN RED CROSS RELIEF

RECAPITULATION OF ACCOUNTS

As of Sept. 1, 1921.

HOUSING AND FEEDING

Kitchen Labor		$1,046.31	
Food	$5,352.64		
Refund	91.07	5,261.57	
Refugee Camp Labor		437.50	
Shelter Labor		392.32	
Lumber & Building Material		4,121.07	
Construction labor		178.60	
Shelter (Tents)		6,142.10	$17,579.47

MEDICAL AND SURGICAL
Care of Riot Sick and Wounded

Emergency Hospital Labor	1,821.37	
Medical Hospital Supplies	1,418.46	
Nurses	3,570.92	
Hospitals (Care of Wounded)	2,834.85	
Hospital Laundry	220.00	
Physicians and Surgeons	5,871.00	
Plumbing and Fittings	1,244.11	16,981.70

FAMILY REHABILITATION

Clothing Commissary Labor		298.01	
Furniture (Cots)		3,308.24	
Blanket Supplies		1,725.51	
Clothing Supplies		982.06	
Kitchen Utensils		278.83	
Household Supplies		1,925.22	
Transportation Persons	4,334.07		
Refund	67.09	4,266.98	
Telegraph & Telephone	230.52		
Refund	14.07	216.45	
Miss Mildred Leslie - Salary		325.00	13,326.30

MISCELLANEOUS

1921 Tulsa Race Riot *"Angels of Mercy"*

(Copy)

Tulsa, Oklahoma
July 1st, 1921

Mr. Maurice Willows

Red Cross Headquarters

Tulsa, Oklahoma.

Kind Sir:

This seems to express to you the profound gratitude, not only of every Negro in Tulsa, but throughout the civilized world wherever there is a negro. Words fail me in trying to express our appreciation for your noble work for us. You and the Great Red Cross are helping us as a race to shut out of our lives all that is evil, to do our "Duty", and in that way we hope to receive the pure, the beautiful, the good, the true, and when the time comes that we shall add our motto to the music of the spheres it will be full of "Joy and Thanksgiving, no harsh note to mar the full, harmonious sound".

> "We have but faith, we cannot know;
> For service is of things we see,
> And yet we trust it comes from Thee,
> A beam in darkness, let it grow."

Knowing that God will reward you for what you have striven to do for us, for what you are doing, and for what you will do; in His words we read that what is done for the least of His subjects is precious in His sight.

Is the prayer of a grateful people,

Very respectfully yours,

(Signed) Louella T. West
and
J. S. West, Pastor
A. M. E. Church

1921 Tulsa Race Riot "Angels of Mercy"

(COPY)

R E S O L U T I O N S

On the 31st night in May, 1921, the fiercest race war known to American history broke out, lasting until the next morning, June 1st, 1921. As a result of the regrettable occurrence, many human lives were lost and millions of dollars worth of property were stolen and burned. Hundreds of innocent negroes suffered as a result of this calamity - suffered in loss of lives, injury from gun-shot wounds, and loss of property. Many of us were left helpless and almost hopeless. We sat amid the wreck and ruin of our former homes and peered listlessly into space. It was at this time and under such conditions that the American Red Cross - that Angel of Love and Mercy - came to our assistance. This great organization found us bruised and bleeding, and like the good Samaritan, she washed our wounds and administered unto us. Constantly, in season and out, since this regrettable occurrence, this great organization, headed by that high class Christian gentleman, Mr. Maurice Willows, has heard our every cry in this our dark hour and has ever extended to us practical sympathy. As best she could, with food and raiment and shelter she has furnished us. And to this great Christian organization our heartfelt gratitude is extended.

Therefore, be it resolved that we, representing the entire colored citizenship of the city of Tulsa, Oklahoma, take this means of extending to the American Red Cross, thru Mr. Willows our heart-felt thanks for the work it has done and is continuing to do for us in this our great hour of need.

Resolved further that a copy of these resolutions be sent to the American Red Cross Headquarters, a copy be mailed to Mr. Willows and his co-workers, and that a copy be spread upon the minutes of the East End Welfare Board.

Respectfully submitted,

(Signed)

B. C. Franklin	I. N. Spears
E. F. Saddler	P. A. Chappelle
J. W. Hughes	Dimpie L. Bush

<u>Committee.</u>

1921 Tulsa Race Riot *"Angels of Mercy"*

Office Of The
EAST END RELIEF BOARD

Tulsa, Oklahoma, December 24, 1921.

The courage with which Tulsa Negroes withstood repeated attempts of the city administration to deliver the "burned area" over to certain land grafters is the subject of most favorable comment all over the country. The rapidity with which business buildings and residences are being rebuilt, in most instances, better than before is proof in wood and brick and in stone, of the black man's ability to make progress against the most cunningly planned and powerfully organized opposition.

Without weakening the above statement and taking nothing from the Tulsa Negroes courage, fortitude and resourcefulness, gratitude forces the admission that had it not been for the helping hand of the American Red Cross Society, his morale would have broken and the splendid history he has made since June 1st, 1921, when the savings of a lifetime were reduced to ashes, would have been impossible. The Red Cross has wrought so nobly in our behalf, is due largely to the spirit of the man in charge, Mr. Maurice Willows. He is an apostle of the square deal for every man, regardless of race or color. Behind closed doors in council with bodies of influential white men, he fought battles and won victories for us sufficient to merit the everlasting gratitude of our people. The Red Cross as a society, has ministered to our physical needs and Mr. Willows, as a man, has stood for our civic rights at home and a fair presentation of our case abroad. When importuned by interested parties to refer to the eventualities of May 31st and June 1st, in his official report, as a "Negro uprising", he stubbornly refused and instead, called it "the Tulsa disaster" and in addition told the truth as, upon investigation, he found it.

While assembled to witness the method by which the Red Cross has elected to give Christmas Cheer to the Negro Children of Tulsa and upon the eve of Mr. Willows' departure from our midst, the undersigned thought it fitting to offer these few words of appreciation on behalf of the entire Negro population of Tulsa, for the unselfish service he has rendered us, with the added assurance that the prayers of a people whom hardship and oppression have thought how to pray will follow him and his associated wherever, in response to the call of suffering humanity and in the line of duty, they may go.

EAST END RELIEF COMMITTEE

Tulsa Tribune, May 31st, 1921

NAB NEGRO FOR ATTACKING GIRL IN AN ELEVATOR

A negro delivery boy who gave his name to the police as "Diamond Dick" but who has been identified as Dick Rowland, was arrested on South Greenwood Avenue this morning, by Officers Carmichael and Pack charged with attempting to assault the 17-year-old white elevator girl in the Drexel building early yesterday.

He will be tried in municipal court this afternoon on a state charge.

The girl said she noticed the negro a few minutes before the attempted assault looking up and down the hallway on the third floor of the Drexel building as if to see if there was anyone in sight but thought nothing of it at the time.

A few minutes later he entered the elevator she claimed, and attached her, scratching her hands and face and tearing her clothes. Her screams brought a clerk from Renberg's store to her assistance and the negro fled. He was captured and identified this morning both by the girl and clerk police say.

Rowland denied that he tried to harm the girl but admitted he put his hand on her arm in the elevator when she was alone.

Tenants of the Drexel building said the girl is an orphan who works as an elevator operator to pay her way through business college.

1921 Tulsa Race Riot *Angels of Mercy*

Statement of one of the Negroes

On the night of May 31st, between nine and ten o'clock, someone told me there was a race conflict. I was asked to go down on the street, but after being told that some had gone to the Court House I refused to go, knowing that I could not use any influence with the scattered bunch. On the morning of June 1st, I arose, expecting to go to the school house. I did not have any idea that the trouble had reached such a proportion.

At five o'clock a whistle was blown, seven aeroplanes were flying over the colored district, and a Machine Gun was placed in front of my home. I was called to the door by home guards and armed citizens. I was not dressed, but was told to bring my family out. They said if we would obey they would protect us and our property. I was not allowed to go back in the house. I called my wife and son, she came out dressed only in a kimona and shoes. We were ordered to put our hands above our heads, marched up Fairview Street, then across the Stand Pipe Hill to Easton Street, where we found automobiles driven by ladies and men.

We were carried to the City Jail, the men were placed in the corridor down stairs, the women were carried up stairs. After so many were crowded into the corridor, we were carried to Convention Hall. Many people cheered and clapped their hands as we were marched four abreast with our hands above our head. A man was shot at the door of the Convention Hall while both hands were above his head. Many men who were shout out in the city were brought in the hall and we heard their cries and groans. Namely: Dr. Jackson, Johnson and Stovall. We looked out of the windows, saw our homes go up in smoke. At noon, we were fed with sandwiches and coffee.

In the last afternoon, we were allowed to leave the Convention Hall only when some white person we had worked for would come and vouch for us. Mr. Oberholtzer, City Superintendent of Public Schools, came and called for all colored teachers, and we were taken to the old City High School, where I met my wife again. All the lady teachers were taken to the homes of the city principals and cared for nicely. We were allowed to stay in the old High School all night. The next morning, I saw my wife much improved as to her dress. Miss Kimble of the Domestic Science Department of the white High School gave us our breakfast.

The next morning, without hat or shoes, I was determined to improve my personal appearance and comfort. After much solicitation I was allowed to go under the guard of a soldier down on Main Street to Renberg's Clothing Store. He gave all the colored male teachers a suit of clothes and hat. In the evening of the first day after the trouble, I was allowed to go out and look over the burned area. Thirty-five blocks, including my home and eight rent houses, were in ashes.

My second night was spent in the Booker T. Washington High School, which had been placed in charge of the Red Cross. Our wives slept on one side of the house on cots and the men on the other side. I was placed temporarily in charge of conditions of the food supply.

We lined the people up, many hundreds being in the line, and fed them their meals by allowing them to pass between two tables, on one was sandwiches, the other, coffee. In this way, we gave each his allowance.

In a very short while, the entire High School Plant was made into a hospital, office rooms, distributing rooms, etc., which soon brought a partial temporary relief to the many who were suffering from wounds, hunger, and the need of clothes.

The stories told by those who came for relief are so freighted with horror, I refrain from repeating them. Many of the sick were forced from home. Those on crutches were compelled to go likewise. A mother giving birth to child was no exception to the rule.

A Reconstruction Committee was appointed by the Mayor of the city. A like committee was ordered selected by his honor from the remaining negro population. We have been asked to give up the lands on which our homes, business, churches and schools were located and requested to go north and east of the city, but and rebuild. The only consideration offered us was leave our lots and when they have increased in value, they will sell them and we have the profit thereby. Thus far, we have failed to acquiesce in the recommendation of the request.

(Signed) J. W. Hughes, Prin. City School.

1921 Tulsa Race Riot "Angels of Mercy"

To Mr. Willows.

A request from a true friend,
As you must leave you do entend;
And your leaving is a gret,
As you have did for us - we can never forget.

Please take this as a token
To all whom may concern,
That you come and went as a gentleman,
And the colored of Tulsa will confirm.

When you far away from Tulsa town,
Do not think of us with a frown,
For God only can tell
How much we appreciate you as well

Thank God for the Red Cross,
For by His hand he put you boss,
And thus He would been to blame
If you and your host had not carried out His aim.
        Amen.

        - A. J. Newman.
           Nov., 1921.

CHRISTMAS TREE

The body of the foregoing report was written prior to the one big event in the lives of the Negro children of the devastated district. For the first time in their lives, these hundreds of little folks were without their former comfortable homes. The resources of their parents had been reduced to a point where Christmas could not mean much to them. The workers of the Red Cross staged for them probably the largest Christmas affair ever staged in Tulsa. A beautiful big tree was placed in front of the Red Cross Relief Headquarters. Mr. Chas. Page of Sand Springs kindly furnished the lighting and decorations. The tree was topped with a large cross.

Imagine, if you can, this huge tree brightly lighted standing on Hartford Street in the middle of a district which had once been comfortable homes, but now filled up with little one and two-room wooden shacks with here and there and everywhere large piles of brick and stone, twisted metal and dabre, reminding one of the horrible fact of last June. War of the worst sort there had been. The Maurice Willows Hospital (named such by unanimous vote of the colored people of the district as a measure of their appreciation for what the Red Cross Director has meant to them) stood within a few yards of where the tree was placed. Imagine, if you can, the job brought to the twenty-seven patients when after dusk on Christmas Eve a chorus of twenty-two hundred voices sang their Christmas carols and typical negro melodies. Never has the writer witnessed more spontaneous outburst of Christmas fervor than on this occasion. Whole families were there - men, women and children. "Swing Low, Sweet Chariot", "Down By the Riber Side", "Standing In The Need Of Prayer", coming from the throats of these people revibrated throughout the night air and attracted most of the crowd gathered in the business section over on Greenwood Street. It seemed as the whole negro population could not resist the chance to sing. A liberal supply of candies, nuts and oranges had been tied up into half-pound packages. Twenty-seven hundred of these were distributed in orderly fashion. Individual packages had been prepared suitable to the needs of women and children. These packages had in them everything in the way of useful articles from a spool of thread to a heating stove. Bed springs, pillows, children's underwear, quilts, cotton bats and every other sort of useful articles were brought by Santa Clause to families which needed these practical things most.

The crowning sentiment of the celebration was in a speech made by one of their leaders who said, "Let us always remember the old negro tradition, 'there is no room in our hearts for hatred'". This occasion furnished what was termed as the "greatest night in the history of Tulsa negroes", and was a fitting culmination of the major relief program of the Red Cross.

The following pages were not included
in Mr. Willows' Official Report, but were submitted
by the Tulsa Chapter of The American Red Cross.
They are included here because of the additional
information they provide.

1921 Tulsa Race Riot "Angels of Mercy"

TULSA CHAPTER

AMERICAN RED CROSS

DISASTER RELIEF

CONDENSED REPORT

Social

Medical

Nursing

Financial

December 31, 1921

NOTE

The following is a brief summary of more detailed reports and historical matter written and compiled for American Red Cross Headquarters at Washington D.C., a copy of which will be filed permanently with the Tulsa County Chapter records.

OFFICERS TULSA CHAPTER RED CROSS

Chairman..A. L. Farmer
Vice Chairman..Clark Field
Chairman Home Service......................................C. E. Buchner
Chairman Home Nursing.........................Mrs. Lilah D. Lindsay
Executive Secretary....................................Mrs. Jennie K. Beam
Treasurer..Alva J. Niles

DIRECTORS

C. E. Buchner	Clint Moore
E. E. Oberholtzer	Phillip Kates
W. F. Stahl	Mrs. Geo. H. Tabor, Jr.
Mrs. John R. Wheeler	W. S. Cochran
Mrs. P. C. West	E. E. Dix
	W. A. Partridge

Director Nursing Service...............................Mrs. W. E. Godfrey

1921 Tulsa Race Riot *"Angels of Mercy"*

December 31st, 1921

TO   Mr. A. L. Farmer, Chairman Executive Committee,
Tulsa County Chapter,
American Red Cross

FROM   Maurice Willows, Director,
Disaster Relief.

On the closing of Relief Operations by the Tulsa Chapter it seems fitting and important to permanently record the activities of the Red Cross, National, Divisional and local, in connection with the Disaster of June 1st, 1921. A detailed narrative and statistical record or history has therefore been compiled and transmitted to your Chapter Secretary.

This record contains:

1. <u>All newspaper accounts of Disaster.</u> These clippings record the activities of the Public Welfare board (original), the National Guard, the Police Department, the Mayor's Reconstruction Committee, the County Commissioners, the Ministerial Association, the Inter-racial Committee and, what is more important, reflect, editorially and otherwise, the consensus of public opinion on question which will inevitably arise in the future for discussion.

2. The Authority placed with Red Cross for the conduct and control of Emergency Relief.

3. A record of problems as they arose and how met.

4. A statement of relationships with other organizations and committees.

5. Photographic evidence of riot scenes, the devastation areas, and of progress in rehabilitation, hospitalization and physical care of riot refugees.

6. Sundry resolutions transmitted to Red Cross by negro organizations.

7. Statistical reports - social and financial.

This record is to voluminous for publication, but is available at Chapter Headquarters for those who may be interested.

THE TULSA DISASTER

of June 1st, 1921, is a matter of local history, know to all Tulsans, and know in part at least, to the rest of the world. This report interests itself with the aftermath - the picking up of the fragments - the relief of human suffering - the care of the sick and wounded, and the bringing order out of chaos. This kind of a task is not spectular, and therefore the local or general public knows too little about it.

During the riotous hours between dawn and noon of a well know June day, what had previously been a prosperous, peaceable and fairly well-ordered negro business and residential district, with a population of approximately twelve thousand negroes - men, women and children, was transferred into a burned and devastated area. Skeletons of brick and stone stood out in ghastly relief against a background of ashes, cinders, twisted iron and steel, charred autos, beds and household implements. Twisted and torn electric wires, gas pipes, meters and other ruined junk was scattered about. A heavy pall of smoke kindly mantled the ruins for the first twenty-four hours, during which time Tulsa had rubbed her eyes and prepared to face a condemning world.

When the smoke had cleared it was found that:

1256   Buildings had been burned

1921 Tulsa Race Riot *"Angels of Mercy"*

314	Buildings (mostly homes) which were spared the torch, were looted and robbed of everything worth while.
10,000	(approximate) persons where homeless
183	Persons were in hospitals, practically all for gunshot wounds or burns.
531	Other persons were seriously enough injured to require first aid medical or surgical care.
0	Were dead, (Figures are omitted for the reason that NO ONE KNOWS.)

PROPERTY LOSSES

A conservative estimate, based upon such data as has become available during a seven months period of relief work, places the losses on buildings, business stocks, household goods and personal property, at three million five hundred thousand dollars. (The only purpose of this estimate is to indicate the approximate size of the economic destruction).

THE AMERICAN RED CROSS AND RELIEF

In a situation such as this, which can better be imagined than described, it is not strange that the community instinctively turned to the American Red Cross.

True, the disaster was not "an act of God". It was "Tulsa made", but the American Red Cross, in accepting responsibility, generously and properly took the position that disaster had visited thousands of human beings, the majority of whom were innocent victims, helpless, and practically sourceless. The "Greatest Mother" could not say no to such a challenge, where human need was so great and human suffering so evident.

In addition to the wholesale destitution, the whole situation was aggravated by the destruction of morale among the victims. Thousands of them were literally frightened out of the city. Large contingent's were found in Sapulpa, Claremore, Muskogee, Oklahoma City, and some were heard from at Kansas City on the north, Los Angeles on the west, Dallas on the south and New York on the east.

The significance of this "scattering" is that the whole relief situation was effected by the wandering of these people and the ultimate return to the site of their old homes, schools, churches and neighbors.

RELIEF PROCESSES

1. The first step was taken when the Mayor of the city placed responsibility for all emergency relief measures on the Red Cross, and in order, the following movements:

2. The quick organization of Red Cross Committees, the detail of which is found in the complete report.

3. The establishment of relief stations. These were located at the Fair Grounds, the Y.M.C.A., McNulty Park, Convention Hall and several of the churches.

4. Making certain the effective hospitalization of the wounded.

5. The establishment of First Aid stations for the care of those not needing hospital care.

    (The newspaper articles and the full report record the measures taken by the State, County and City governments and other civic organizations, all of which carried a share of responsibility for safe-guarding life, limb, and property, following the day of the riot.)

ENTRY OF NATIONAL RED CROSS OFFICIALS

On the morning of the third day following the riot, Mr. Maurice Willows, then Assistant Manager of the Southwestern Division, had, by prearrangement over long distance telephone, reported for duty. After hurried conferences with local Chapter Officials, the Mayor, the Public Welfare Board and others, the direction of relief activities was placed in his hands. Within another twenty-four hours all relief measures had been coordinated and permanent relief headquarters were opened at the Booker T. Washington school. Concurrently with this centralization, the churches, the Y.M.C.A. and other temporary relief places were evacuated. After thorough office organization, the first sizeable task was a survey of the negro homes remaining in the district and the servants quarters throughout the city by a field staff of Red Cross Nurses quickly mobilized for the purpose. Briefly the results of this survey was as follows:

No. of calls made by Nurses.	4512
No. of patients found needing medical or nursing care	551
Classified as follows:	
1. Maternity cases needed care	38
2. Infants and children needing care	369
3. Other physical breakdowns needing care	154

Of these 80 were sent to the dispensary for care. Definite nursing care was given to 84, and continuing nursing care was given to 169 people in their temporary homes. (A detailed list of nurses is given in the detail report).

VACCINATION

Immediately following this survey it was deemed of importance to use the utmost precautions against epidemic. Especially important did it seem to administer serum to the detention camp refugees. It was necessary to corral all available vaccine and typhoid serum. Approximately 1800 refugees were treated by the physicians of the city who were organized for the purpose.

Chronologically for medical and nursing phase of the relief work was as follows:

1. Immediate surgical and medical care of the wounded at six private hospitals.
2. The mobilization of all available nurses for hospitals and field service.
3. Placing the State Supervisor of the Red Cross Nursing in charge.
4. The organization of a committee of doctors under whose direction the state supervisor was to supervise.
5. The mobilization of vaccine and the typhoid serum and the administering of same to the refugees.
6. A Field Survey of Public Health Nurses.
7. The equipping of a First Aid station, a general Dispensary and a V. D. Clinic.
8. Equipping and furnishing a central hospital.
9. The evacuation of the private hospitals.

WORK DURING SUMMER MONTHS

Along with the foregoing set-up for medical and surgical care, the social relief work was quickly and thoroughly organized with a staff of trained family workers in charge, assisted by an able corp of volunteers, the work of which is described in detail in the detailed history.

THE FAMILY RELIEF WORK

Thus the whole organization quickly settled down to a long time schedule for relief activities. Naturally the first big task was that of HOUSING. Immediately following the disaster, the solution lay in three directions: First, the use of crowding of a certain number into servants quarters throughout the white district. Second, the use of detention camps. Third, the quick construction of tents and equipment. At the end of the first week, 184 tents had been equipped as temporary homes. The next move following the first housing was to make these tents liveable for families.

Sufficient progress had been made by the first of July to warrant the evacuation of the Fair Grounds, which had from the beginning been ably administered by a staff of local workers under the direction of Mr. Newt Graham of the Exchange Trust Company.

SLOW PROGRESS DURING SUMMER MONTHS

A volume of local history might be written regarding the serious details and obstructions in the rehabilitation program, the causes for which revolved around the lack of action of the public authorities who were charged with the responsibility of working out a reconstruction program for the city and county. In this connection it will be recalled that a serious blunder occurred when the first "Public Welfare Board" chosen by the Chamber of Commerce and which had authority during the first days following the trouble was declared out of commission and a new "Reconstruction Committee" was appointed by the Mayor.

The first committee had a program outlined; the second committee had none, and from all evidence the second committee, after seven months inactive service, evolved no constructive plans. It will also be recalled that part of the burned area lay within the city limits, and part of it in the county outside the city limits. The period from June until October 1st proved to be a sloughing off period, during which time the negroes within the city limits were practically forbidden to help themselves by rebuilding wooden houses of any sort. It was not until the courts made certain decisions in September that the negroes were allowed to replace their temporary tent homes with wooden shacks. This delay of three months consequently retarded all other concurrent relief measures.

Addendum

I want to thank Robert Powers and his staff at the Tulsa Historical Society for their kind cooperation. They have been very helpful to this first time publisher.

For more information on the history leading to and following the Tulsa Race Riot, I strongly recommend the very well researched, "Death in A Promised Land," by Scott Ellsworth, published in 1982.

I thank Mr. Ellsworth for encouraging my publication, and for these kind words:

"In the great tragedy that was the Tulsa race riot, no single organization did more to ease the pain and suffering than the American Red Cross. Maurice Willows' well-written official report not only sheds light on one of the nation's darkest days, but tells a true story of courage and compassion in the face of overwhelming catastrophe."

Scott Ellsworth, author of
Death in a Promised Land:
The Tulsa Race Riot of 1921

ADDENDUM

"The 1921 Tulsa Race Riot-Angels of Mercy," is a compilation of material from the memorabilia collection of Red Cross Relief Director, Maurice Willows. The following was not a part of that collection, but is included here because it might answer the often asked question, "What became of Dick Rowland and Sarah Page, the couple in the alleged elevator incident, after she refused to file charges and he was exonerated?"

Ruth Sigler Avery, who witnessed the Tulsa Riot as a seven year old child, answers that question in her forthcoming documentary, "Fear, the Fifth Horseman." Over the years Ms. Avery has interviewed many riot witnesses. Her book is a collection of those interviews, including one with Dick Rowland's "mother."

Here, with Ms. Avery's permission, is that interview. Ms. Avery believes it to be true.

1921 Tulsa Race Riot "Angels of Mercy"

AFRICAN - AMERICAN DAMIE ROWLAND FORD -ORAL HISTORY "MOTHER OF DICK ROWLAND" ON JULY 22, 1972

On July 22, 1972, Ruth Avery interviewed Damie Rowland Ford, owner and manager of the Beech Hotel on Greenwood Ave. Up two flights of narrow stairs, I turned the corner, and met 87-year-old Mrs. Damie Rowland Ford using the crutch she had used since she had polio during her childhood. She was a tiny, wrinkled, black woman wearing a white dotted-swiss cap over her grey hair. In her apartment, she proudly showed me the diamond ring her husband had given her when they were married. "He always called me his little doll", she said. Then she began to tell me the story of the little boy, Jimmie Jones, whom she had raised.

"There were four members of my Rowland family who came from Texas to Muskogee, Oklahoma before statehood. Mom and Pop, who was known as Reverend Clarence. He died in 1919, and is buried in Tulsa. I, just like Mr. Ford had a fourth-grade education, but I wanted to be out on my own."

"I worked in servile positions until I got a little money ahead. Then I started running my own cafe in Cushing, Oklahoma. I married Mr. Ford, and then later divorced him. After that, I moved to Vinita, Oklahoma.

"One day outside my one-room grocery store (the living room of my house) I saw a skinny, little, barefoot, black boy come into the store who was almost smothered wearing his only garment, a big man's shirt. He looked like he was about six-years-old. 'I'm hungry,' he said. I fixed him a sandwich, and gave him some milk. He had a winsome way of catering to me when I went out later and sat out in my rocker under the trees. I had just gotten over the flu. He said that he would help me regularly if I wanted him to just for food to eat. Then he fetched me water and played at my feet. Then we just visited together for an hour or so."

"I found out during our conversation that he was an orphan named Jimmie Jones, and he had only two sisters, with no other relatives at all. The three children lived on the streets in Vinita, sleeping wherever they could, and begging for food that was given to them by people that lived in houses, or from strangers who gave them money.

"I had him go right then and bring his two older sisters to me. I asked them if I couldn't take care of Jimmie from then on. He could help me, and I would feed and take care of him just like as mother. I liked the idea of having a boy around to do work in my store, and be company for me. My parents were still in Muskogee."

"They said, 'Yes, for that would mean just one less mouth to feed.' And that is how I became Jimmie's 'Mama.' We worked together in the store, and he slept at night on a pallet in my dining room. The living room was where I had the grocery store, and I had a one-bedroom, a bath, and small kitchen-dining room."

"A year or so later, I decided to move to Tulsa, and bring my Mama and Daddy from Muskogee to live with us. Daddy died and was buried in 1919 in Tulsa. I always called her 'Mama,' so Jimmy began to call her the same name, and began calling me 'Aunt Damie'.

"When Jimmy started to school, he changed and registered under his favorite name Dick. He got along fine in elementary grades, and was a big help to Mama and me throughout the years.

"After Mama died, I bought a one-story building and rented out rooms for a living. Dick used to clean the rooms up for me after the tenants moved out. He didn't stay around home too much. He worked at odd jobs to help make us some extra money."

"Then, in the second year in high school, he wasn't too good a student, for he began running around with the wrong kind of crowd. He played football and then would drop out of school to return the next year at football season. Then he finally dropped out altogether. He got jobs to work wherever he could."

"However, he always seemed to always have plenty of money to spend, I noticed. Once, he purchased himself a birthday present, a diamond ring of which he was very proud. Some of his friends nick-named him 'Diamond Dick'. That pleased him."

"I often thought since he ran around with both black and white people that mixed- up down on First Street which was where Tulsa's 'red-light' district was, and I thought that he might be breaking the law, but he never told me so. He seemed to know a lot of white girls that lived down on or near First Street. He talked about one of his new friends, Sarah Page, a white girl, who was two years younger than he."

When Dick was seventeen years-of-age, he got a job as a bootblack in the Ingersol Recreation Parlor on the northeast corner of Third and Main Streets in Tulsa. He worked with another young fella, Robert Fairchild, who was the other bootblack."

"Dick received a lot of money from tips given him by oil men when they had their shoes shined. He was nice-looking, light-brown ,had a winning personality, and was very jovial. He was about five -foot -ten-inches tall, well-built, and weighed about one hundred and seventy pounds. He gave me money regularly from his tips to help pay for our expenses."

"One Monday noon, the 30th of May, he came running home, breathless, and said that the police were after him for what had just occurred."

"He said he had just delivered some shoes upon the third floor of the Drexel building to a customer, had used the building's restroom, and when leaving, he got into Sarah Page's elevator to go down. But she hadn't gotten the elevator even with the floor, so he tripped and stepped on her instep. She was so mad at him for stepping on her sore foot that she pounded him again and again on the top of his head with her leather purse, vigorous enough to break off its handles."

"He said, 'I reached up to hold her arms back and prevent her pounding my head, and held them there. When the elevator reached the ground floor lobby, Sarah screamed, I've been assaulted!' A clerk came running out from Renberg Clothiers right next to the elevator shaft, and started to try to catch me. I outran him, and fled here. I've gotta hide until tomorrow.'

"We pulled our blinds down, and I insisted that he stay at home the rest of the day. But on Tuesday, May 31st, he wanted to go join some friends. He didn't come back that night, and I was very bothered."

"He called me. He said he had been arrested on the street by two black police officers, H. C. Pack and Henry Carmichael. He was in the city jail on Second Street, and he pleaded with me to get him an attorney."

"I went down and talked with Sheriff McCullough, and upon his recommendations, I hired Wash Hudson, a prominent white Tulsa attorney, to defend him. He was hired by the court, so it wouldn't cost me anything, which was fine with me."

"That Tuesday afternoon, I heard that they had transferred him to the Tulsa County Jail at Sixth and Boulder for safe keeping for there was talk on the street of lynching him."

"I didn't see Dick again until weeks later. He told me at that time that Sheriff McCullough had secreted him out from the county jail late that Tuesday afternoon, and had driven him to Kansas City, Kansas to stay with some friends of Sarah's. That was were she had lived with her husband that she had divorced."

"The riot happened that night of May 31st. I lost my rooming house at 505 East Archer. The loss of the building was around $5,000. I had nothing except the clothes on my back, so I stayed with some friends just outside of Tulsa for the next few days."

"When I returned the Chamber of Commerce issued me a tent, and it was put on top of the ashes where my home had been."

"Dick came to see me only once after he moved to Kansas City. He said Sarah Page had moved up there with him for she had felt terrible that the police had arrested him. She had refused to press charges against him. The charges of assault had been made to the police by the Renberg's clerk, and they had to look Sarah up later at her home off First Street to identify Dick. My attorney, Wash Hudson, told me that all charges of assault had been dropped."

"Dick wrote me every month or so while he lived in Kansas City, Kansas, and kept me up on the news about his life. Then he moved to the state of Oregon. He wrote me after he left Kansas City, and was settled in Oregon. He told me that Sarah Page was still 'bummin' around in Kansas City.

"Dick worked at the shipyards in various towns along the Oregon coast, and continued to write me throughout the years. I was the only relative that he knew of, for we never heard from his sisters after he had moved in with me as a child."

"Then, just a few years ago, I ceased getting any mail from him. One day I got a letter from his room-mate advising me that Dick had been killed in an accident there on the wharf in Oregon. Dick had told this friend that I was the only relative he had, and had given him my address. He had never married. So that was the end of my boy."

END NOTES *(by Ruth Avery)*

1. This account was verified in a story appearing in the Tulsa World June 1st which relates that Sara Page was walking down Third Street, and had run into a friend of hers.
   After telling her what happened, Sara showed her friend the purse with both handles broken off which had occurred when she pounded Dick over the head in the elevator in anger.

2. Washington Elias Hudson was one of the most outstanding members of the Klu Klux Klan when he served as President of the Oklahoma State Senate when over fifty percent of the State Legislature were members of *The Invisible Kingdom*.

**You may order additional copies of
"The 1921 Tulsa Race Riot-Angels of Mercy," by email or Fax.**

**email: bhower@fullnet.net or auslande@swbell.net
Fax: (918) 743-3863 or (918) 834-2572**

The author has described "The 1921 Tulsa Race Riot-Angels of Mercy," as the only publication telling the story "in the words of those who lived through and reported on it," showing copies of the original documents from which those words came.

There is another publication which tells the story in the words of an eyewitness journalist, Mary E. Jones Parrish, titled "Race Riot 1921 Events of the Tulsa Disaster." It includes "testimonials" of some eyewitnesses, but does not show the source documents. It is most interesting however, and recommended reading.